SONGS OF LUST AND LOVE

(A Book of Poems)

Musings on Intimacy of Human Love
~ Scriptural Interpretation ~

LALITHA IYER

Edited by

Dr Tapan Kumar Pradhan

CONTENT

BOOK – 1

PART – I : The Secret Sutras

PART - II : An Eyeful of Lust

PART - III : Sounds of Love

BOOK – 2

PART - VII : The Four Seasons

PART – VIII : Sex & Sin

PART - IX : Kiss of Life

PART – X : Temple of Love

ACKNOWLEDGEMENT

I owe a deep debt of gratitude to my fellow poet friends on Poemhunter.com website. My poetic craft has been shaped by the honest feedback received from thousands of readers. Although I have published my poems on several online platforms, it is on poemhunter.com that I received wholehearted support from many kindred souls.

Dr Tapan Kumar Pradhan offered to present my poems in a book form. Many years ago I had requested Dr Tapan to write a few poems for me. I had also once requested him to gift a book of his choice to me. He had promised to me both. I think he has far exceeded my expectations. I have discussed with him several of my poems at length. I have also discussed with him the underlying unity among all the major religions of the world including Christianity, Hinduism and Islam. I believe that he shares my thoughts on the relevance of ancient teachings on love and sex for the modern world. I have full faith in his capacity to honestly interpret my poems.

LALITHA IYER

FOREWORD

This book contains one hundred and sixty poems exploring the depths of human love spread over ten different themes. Although the book treats the subject of love and lust, it is not vulgarly erotic in its approach. Underneath the titillatingly erotic content, the book explores the underlying spiritual foundation of the human emotion of romantic love. The uniqueness of this book lies in the depiction of human love from the perspectives of five senses, four seasons and three major world religions.

According to the poet, the natural attraction between man and woman is a reflection of the universal love force immanent in all creation. Marriage of two adults through mutual consent is not only a holy sacrament, but also a divine form of worship of God in human form. True love finds fulfilment through the covenant of betrothal and marriage. Culmination of passionate love is also expressed through the birth of a divine love child.

Many of these poems have a definite autobiographical undertone. The poet's own life experiences have been depicted through symbolic expressions. The book traces the poet's journey from her initial disenchantment with sense enjoyment in pursuit of romantic passion to her gradual awakening to the existence and possibility of selfless true love lurking behind the external clouds of materialistic desire and suffering.

Lalitha Iyer is an outstanding poet-scholar with an unconventional style and consummate mastery of English language. She has expertly depicted finer nuances of erotic love through skillful use of words and imagery. For deeper appreciation of her craft, the reader may like to read these poems again and again. Lalitha's poems are highly symbolic and they powerfully convey the eternal spiritual truths contained in world scriptures like the Vedas, Upanishads, Bible and Quran. This book presents her scholarly poems along with relevant passages from the scriptures and ancient spiritual texts.

Lalitha has written thousands of poems in different languages. This book is a humble attempt to bring the best amongst her magnificent oeuvre under a single comprehensive framework. I have selected these poems on the basis of their immediate relevance to the overall theme and structure of this book. These need not be the most representative of Lalitha's immense poetic output.

In some of the poems the poet has provided explanatory notes to throw light on the background of the composition. Occasionally I have provided additional footnotes to drive home the biographical context as well as the spiritual undertones of a poem. My notes essentially contain my views, and need not reflect the poet's original views on the matter.

Many of the poems have been edited to conform to the overall design of the book. Some poems had originally been composed in free flowing passage form. These have been tweaked slightly so as to have a more presentable verse form. I have been in close correspondence with the poet for almost a decade. So I have reason to believe that I understand the poet's point of view behind these creations. I am thankful to the poet for allowing me the liberty to freely explore and interpret these spiritual gems.

Some of the poems contained in this book have appeared in slightly different versions on various websites and online platforms. The poet has also been editing and tweaking her poems online from time to time. However, I am presenting the poems as received by me from the poet during my extensive correspondence.

In my extended online correspondence with the poet, I used to address her affectionately as "Lolita". Lalitha Iyer and I myself had jointly composed around 200 poems on the Lolita theme. I have provided snippets of those exchanges at certain places in the book to provide context to the poems.

EDITOR

INTRODUCTION

Love is the most powerful among all human emotions. It is the primary force that attracts people and keeps communities, societies and nations together. However when it comes to romantic sexual attraction between a man and a woman, the same love force is often considered as something unholy and is even frowned upon. It is a paradox beyond commonsense reasoning!

Ancient Hindu scriptures like Veda and Upanishads have been very liberal about human sexuality. However, comparatively modern scriptures like Bible and Quran appear to have a more conservative puritanical attitude towards sex. Or at least they have been interpreted that way. Bible depicts sexual attraction as the "fall of man". Quran has also depicted many forms of sexual activities as immoral.

In matters of love and sex, the Hindu worldview is starkly different from the Islamic and Christian worldview. For Hindus sex is not a sin, but rather a celebration of life. Of course, in the traditional four goals of life (Dharma, Artha, Kama, Moksha), Hindus place Kama (sexual desire) at the lowest rung. But sexual longing has never been associated with sinfulness in ancient Hindu scriptures.

There has been debates over sex for procreation and sex for recreation. Many puritan Hindus quote some scriptures to prescribe sex only for progeny (पुत्रार्थं क्रीयते भार्या). But authentic Vedic texts have prescribed sex for pleasure without progeny (Brihad 6.4.10). Even Kama Sutra prescribes sex only for pleasure. The various postures and love games described in Kama Sutra are intended to maximise that pleasure alone.

Although sex during menstruation is prohibited in Quran, the Hindu Upanishads do not explicitly prohibit it. However, both Vedic texts and Quran attach "uncleanliness" to the natural phenomenon of menstruation.

Spiritual Foundation of Human Love

According to Hindu scriptures, the sexual act is one of the highest form of worship of the divine. Couples engaging in intimate sexual relations have been exhorted to regard each other's sexual organs as tools of fire sacrifice rituals. The male and female body organs are to be visualised as manifestations of cosmic principles. People who perform sexual act as a form of divine worship receive highest spiritual benefits from it, whereas those who engage in sex without understanding its spiritual significance derive no merit from it. This is the essence of Hindu philosophy on human lust and love.

Boundless joy is human soul's default nature. Due to attachment to sense organs and objects of sensory enjoyment, human soul becomes forgetful of its true divine nature. However the soul subconsciously remembers its connection with the cosmic reality. The separation from its divine origin makes the soul long for human connections. All carnal desires for sense gratification are external manifestation of the soul's longing for divine connection through forgetfulness. Inner spiritual journey starts with one's understanding of the primal cause of one's physical and emotional longing. Constant meditation, self-purification and sacrifices help in gradual removal of the veils of ignorance from the lover's mind.

Lalitha's Poetry

The present volume contains one hundred and sixty poems by the enigmatic poet Lalitha Iyer depicting human love in its myriad dimensions. These include poems on love, sex, lust, passion and longing. However, the eroticism depicted in Lalitha's poetry are less about carnal passion, and more about the celebration of human love in divine joy. The erotic imagery in this volume are highly symbolic. They have a clear underlying philosophy, which the reader would like to fathom through repeated reading and close attention to details.

Although these poems explore depths of human love, Lalitha is by no means just a lovey-dovey "romantic" poet. She has penned hundreds of poems on human sorrow and pain also. She has even written extensively on philosophy, religion and social issues. Her haunting poems on human sorrow have been separately published under the title "Songs of Sadness". Even in the present volume the discerning reader can see glimpses of her philosophical insight while describing human love and lust.

Scope of the Book

The 160 poems in this volume have been arranged under ten different parts, each showcasing a different dimension of human love.

Part-I is titled "Secrets of the Sutras". The poems in this part make a comparison of the treatment of human sexuality in the scriptures of major world religions like Christianity, Islam and Hinduism. Much of the reference has been made to Kama Sutra by Sage Vatsyayana and Chapter-6 of Brihadaranyaka Upanishad. Poems like "Hymen Truths" and "Hymen's Song" convey the feministic standpoint through powerful visual imagery. "Flesh Absorber" and "Come Rape Me" throw challenge to male chauvinism. "Poly Love" is a take on widespread secret practice of polygamy. Poems like "Enigmatic Navel", "Leaning Tower of Pissah" and "Eunuch Love" etc use *double entendre* to convey an idea.

The next five parts describe the manifestation of love through the five senses of sight, sound, touch, taste and smell. Part-II titled "An Eyeful of Lust" deals with visual cues in human love. The most representative poems in this part are "Beauty of Curves" and "Picture of Plunging Trips. Another poem "Tipsy Eyes and Crimson Thighs" depicts the visual attraction for opposite gender. However the last poem in this part titled "Love at the End of Tunnel" indicates that the poet is actually searching for true love beneath the façade of optical illusion of carnal attraction.

Part-III is titled "Sounds of Love". This part contains poems depicting the emotion of love experienced through the agency of speech, sound and hearing. The poems "I Hear Monsoon's Knocks" and "A Leaf Whispers on My Body Tree" vividly express the sound vibrations associated with erotic desire. "The Mating Call" likens a cuckoo's love call to an arrow's shot. The final few poems in this part titled "Sound of Thought" explores the possibility of hearing the lover's feelings without the exchange of words.

Part-IV titled "Touch of the Wild" deals with the tactile sensation of love. The poems "He Loves and Licks" and "Voltage of Your Touch" are quite representative. "Tugging at My Skirt" and "Bathe My Body in Love" in a titillating manner depict the role of human touch in evoking passion.

Part-V is titled "Forbidden Fruits". The poems in this section depict love through the sense of Taste. Poems like "My Body Ice Cream" and "May I Taste Your Sun Lips" evoke images of the human tongue expressing the intimate emotions. "Taste of Our First Kiss" metaphorically points to the first real contact with God's omnipresent love.

Part-VI titled "The Perfume Garden" explores the experience of human love through the sense of smell. The poems "Secret Fragrance of Love" and "Odor of Your Manly Sweat" showcase the poet's ability to evoke raw sexuality through picture words. The poem "Musk of Eden" clearly shows that the poet is not seeking gratification of sensual desires but the noble fulfilment of her inner longings.

Part-VII is titled "The Four Seasons". The poems in this section showcase the different shades of love in different seasons. "Blushing Under Sun Kisses" and "Summer Calls" depict emotions in summer, while poems like "Rain Wet Nights" and "Rain Bride of Desire" evoke monsoon images. "Bride of Winter Passion" simultaneously evokes feelings of frigidity and turbidity in love. "Fertility Dreams in Rain" conveys the emptiness in human love making unless it results in birth of an offspring. Metaphorically it means that all human strivings are futile unless they lead to spiritual awakening.

Part-VIII is titled "Sex and Sin". The eponymous first poem reveals the hypocrisy in human love. "Love in Oval Office" shows the guilt consciousness inherent in forbidden carnal liaisons. "Oo Ma Doggie" and "Homo Erectus" allude to irregular sexual practices. "If Love Not Given" alludes to the controversial Upanishadic message that a woman can be forcibly taken if she does not yield to love.

Part-IX titled "Kiss of Life" dwells extravagantly on the physical act of human kiss through lips. But inwardly they point to blossoming of positive spiritual energies. Poems like "Kiss Me Now" and "I Shall Kiss Them Blind" show the urgency in the poet's longing. "Come Kiss Me" is a satire on the modern campus love.

The culminating Part-X is titled "Temple of God". Poems in this part reflect the poet's growing realisation that unconscious distance from God was her real cause of emotional torment during the earlier phases of her romantic awakening. The poem "Telepathic Love" indicates that the poet seeks depth of love through platonic union. The poem "After Ages I Find a Man" suggests that the poet was seeking an idealistic human companion who would help her to attain her true inner potential instead of exploiting her external sexuality. The penultimate poem "Love at the End of Tunnel" indicates an awakening from carnal desires to the possibility of eternal soul love. The very last poem in the book "You Are My Temple, Lord" reveals the spiritual undercurrents running through the entire book. The poet's carnal passion is completely transmuted into divine longing.

The Epilogue presents revealing facts regarding the true identity of Lalitha Iyer, the enigmatic poet of this volume. Most readers would find it quite shocking, to say the least. But I thought it was my duty to disclose the identity of this truly world class poet, so that people worldwide can appreciate the extraordinary range of the poet's compositions.

Literary Style

Lalitha is a revolutionary poet with a breathtakingly magnificent range. She has a very unique style of poetic expression which stands her apart from other poets in contemporary world literature. This consists essentially in her unbridled freedom in the use of language. Her writing style is refreshingly free from the constraints of traditional grammar. Readers can find such unconventional words and expressions like "hormoned with life", "gayless", "bleeded" and "yesternight" in her poetry. She even describes the process of sexual reproduction of an embryo with words like "spermovumed". She regularly uses the small "i" to denote herself in first person singular to underplay the role of individual ego in the creative process. She coins words like "childer" instead of using conventional expressions like "more childish". All these are her own spontaneous innovations, which do not yet appear in the English dictionary.

Many of her poems almost look like social media posts. She frequently uses SMS and Tweet type abbreviations like u for You, r for Are, hv for Have and gn tc for Good Night, Take Care etc. Often the same poem has her protagonist speak in past, present and future tenses simultaneously. She also deliberately misspells words for special effect – e.g. Mangoose for Mongoose. One never knows for sure whether a particular word in her poem has an inadvertent spelling error, or whether it is deliberately misspelt. Editing her works therefore is an immense challenge, since it is difficult to decide whether to rectify an apparent error, or to just leave them like that!

Tapan Kumar Pradhan

BOOK ONE

THE SECRET SUTRAS

AN EYEFUL OF LUST

SOUNDS OF LOVE

TOUCH ME NOT

FOBIDDEN FRUITS

THE PERFUME GARDEN

A NEW KIND OF LOVE

A new born child
is like this

doesn't know a world does exist,
in any case what a world it is
not known 'tis bliss

she winks and wakes
and then has a shake
of nubile young legs
asks for milk
she awakes O miss

the mist of darkness has been wiped away
the sunrises like each and every day
and the galaxy and moon go away
then it's only my life and yours all say

come love me now
the light is around
from darkness and deep slumber
we have woken
enlightenment ensues
for me and you

Behold!

PART - I

THE SECRET SUTRAS

LOVE IN THE SCRIPTURES

*Then he embraces her
repeating the following mantra:*

*"I am the vital breath and you are speech
You are speech and I am the vital breath.*

*I am Sama and you are Rig
I am heaven and you are earth
Come, let us strive together
so that we may have a child."*

Then he spreads apart her thighs
repeating the following mantra:

*"Spread yourselves apart
Like Heaven and Earth."*

*Inserting his member in her
and joining mouth to mouth,
he strokes her three times head to foot
repeating the following mantra:*

*"Let Vishnu make your womb capable of bearing
Let Tvashtra shape limbs of the child
Let Prajapati pour in the semen
Let Dhatra support the embryo
O Goddess whose glory is widespread
Make her conceive!
May the two Atvins, garlanded with lotuses
support the embryo!
let the two Atvins chum the womb
with two golden arani sticks!*

*I am placing a seed in your womb
to be delivered in the tenth month
as the earth has fire in its womb
as heaven is pregnant with the sun
as the quarters are impregnated by air
so I am impregnating you
by placing this seed in your womb."*

(Brihadaranyaka Upanishad 6.4.20-22)

LOVE IN THE ACT

If a poet is not romantic
if he has not done that
what you call sin
yet do it daily
beneath lingerie
what shall he preach
for painters and poets
women must strip

and then only see
what inspiration
you can beget
to be a poet painter perfect

to be able to visualise
what within veils and veils
of clothing lies

how can you compare
a rose with a lotus
how will you smell
her real fragrance
and enjoy aromas
unless you have enjoyed
a woman's skill

No, not in lust alone
but love true
followed by lust too

else what kind of a poet
will ever be you

unless you have your mind
totally juiced
and lovely desires
induced
only then can you be
a poet like me
ask me not

what sex and sin is
all of you must not
hypocrites be
love a woman then see
how poetry flows
from you to me

"He spreads apart her thighs, repeating the mantra: 'Spread yourselves apart, heaven and earth'. Then inserting his member in her and joining mouth to mouth, he strokes her three times from head to foot, repeating the mantra: 'Let Vishnu make the womb capable of bearing a son! Let Tvashtra shape the limbs of the child! Let Prajapati pour in the semen! Let Dhatra support the embryo! O Goddess whose glory is widespread, make her conceive! May the two Ashvins, garlanded with lotuses, support the embryo!" (Brihadaranyak Upanishad 6.4.21)

"Many mortals, brahmins only in name, perform the sexual act without knowledge of what has been said and depart from this world impotent and without merit." (Brihad. 6.4.4)

WHY HACK MY SHE

I can be bare and nude
Why do hush-hush eye scallop
My moony chaste boobs
I can strip off veil for revel
Egressing 'no-bra-looks'.

Why scope scoop tangently lips
Tint red from beguiling xx blood
Just to satiate your lip hunger?

Why itching psychically in
Nibble nimble young thighs
And triangle in between?
Dive dip deep in horripillant
Ganga Yamuna mating point
I can lay bedecking billow bed

Stop hacking
Stop itching
Stop scooping
Stop scoping

Hey come bare nude
Together for sure
Flush all impure
Into unmarred pure
Why hack then my She?

"O King, there is itching for sex in all beings. Penis of man expands, so
also vulva of woman. The woman and man, getting mad, are then united.
Due to rubbing of one body with another, there is a momentary pleasure…"

(Padma Purana V.100.69-77)

MERMAID WITHOUT A BIKINI

When two angels love
gentle soft and smooth
as roses petals
one would wish
were placed in one's
basket of love daily
by friends equally lovely

I am that fish
with a mermaid's stance
my face is worthy
of many a glance

My mane is like a horse's
and my figure stout
on horseback with a hat on
when I am out

Then as I swim
like a mermaid too
without a bikini
wonder how would you
Life is a melody of much hue
when someone is in love
with someone anew.

"If she is willing, he should proceed, uttering the mantra: 'I transmit reputation into you,' and they both become reputed." (Brihadaranyak Upanishad 6.4.8)

BUTTERFLY ME

A beautiful butterfly
has the privilege of entry
to any nectarish orifice

Hold me, churn me
with your love stick
juice me up sticky
with

let it be plenty
flowery
butter fly
will love to their die
even if it be a candle flame
butterflies love
the burning game
and put all humans
to tearful shame

are you now
at least game
O! what a shame
just hide your name....

"O messenger, the organs of generation of the male and also of the female throb. Then the male and the female, being inflamed with passion, unite. The body of male is rubbed with body of female. Due to coitus a momentary pleasure is produced..." (Padma II.53.98-109)

HETERO SAPIENS SAPIENS

Cogito ergo sum
I know
Therefore I want
The other

Split into two
Like labial walls
Fleshy petals
I long
For
My missing half

Like dark roots
Locked in a pea
A claw at myself
To break free
Of my own trap

I know
Therefore I seek
My other half

"And Allah made of him two **sex**es, male and female." (سورة القيامة, Al-Qiyaama 75.39)

"He was not happy. He desired a mate. So he became as big as a man and woman embracing each other. Then he split himself into two. From that came husband and wife. Therefore this body is one half of oneself, like one of the two halves of a split pea. And then he united with her." (Brihad 6.4.2)

HYMEN TRUTHS

Delicate
Membrane
Hymen
Hi men
Rupture
Torture
Make
It
Rot
Raw
Rendezvous
Of
Libido
Why?

=) -

Its
Psychic
Somatic
Aeonian
Bruise
Blast

==)) -

Vicariously
Suffers
Mother
Mary.

===))) -

Forget

Why
Its
Omni
Mother
((^))
Spot
That
Delivered
All
Flora
Fauna

Universally?!

"Prajapati thought, 'Well, let me make an abode for it,' and he created woman." (Brihadaranyak Upanishad 6.4.2)

HUMOUR STICK

huuuumorrrwristickkkk
does she,
your wifey
wield
an iron
STICK?

accept it
espresso
will do...

after wards
have a
tot or two

under the bed sheet
milk will be free

as if you
are still having
her home made
coffee

try and tell me
I AM GETTIN
the stick freely
almost daily
I still love it
do try and say

Bless me, i.e. you,
I mean you
bless me man!
for the trick
of stick
I share
with fellow drinkers

Shhhhh secret
kindly keep it
Until I come
On my own
Humoured
Powered
Centrifuged
By your stick!

"Then he embraces her, repeating the mantra:- I am the vital breath and you are speech. You are speech and I am the vital breath. I am Sama and you are Rig; I am heaven and you are earth. Come, let us strive together so that we may have a progeny." (Brihadaranyak Upanishad 6.4.20)

HYMEN'S SONG

Candle light oscillating
Luxing like amoeba
Silenced to actuate
Jus Primae Noctis
Right of First Night
Poor just married Dona
Lying like log to
Endure engulf forced
Somatic n' psychic
Defloration harpooning
It's bonking by law. [Shame]

>>==========)) - ((^))

Modern day scoundrels'
Anti-social virile DNA
Actively augmented by
Vile androgenic vaccine
As it is still necessary
For lustful male flocks
Law books read
Its rape unlawful [Odium]

>>==========)) - ((^))

Psychic and somatic
Hymen stay traumatized
Galvanized stigma
Guaranteed to Dona to
Bear blaster blister rest of life.

>>==========))) - ((^))

Has 21st century civilization
Progressed a pico centimeter
From maleficent medieval
Septicemic scenario?

>>==========)) - ((^))

What next - any guesses
For sure atavistic retrograde
Evolution in civilization
To medieval malevolency.

>>==========))) - ((^))

Hi men for hymen assault
women spit on cruddy civilization
Hey all join in mass spitting
Kicking whapping bashing on
Twin balls [OO] of live carnal cadaver
As Poet Taslima Nasrin did
On this de-civilized society

>>==========))) - ((^))

"Her vulva is the sacrificial ground; her pubic hair is the sacred grass; her labia majora are the Soma-press; and her labia minora are the fire blazing at the centre. A man who engages in sexual intercourse with this knowledge obtains as great a world as a man who performs a Soma sacrifice, and he appropriates to himself the merits of the women with whom he has sex. The women, on the other hand, appropriate to themselves the merits of a man who engages in sexual intercourse with them without this knowledge. (Brihadaranyak Upanishad 6.4.3)

ENIGMATIC NAVEL

Ooh-la-la
Why cave navel?
Oi-amma oi-amma
Unveil
Navigate I'll
Keep not enigmatic.
Your enigmatic navel
A makeshift
From mother fixation
Of neonatehood
To fiancée fixation
Of youngwomanhood
Is my visual cuddle.
Put on low waist jeans
Tattoo butterfly around
Decor with diamond
Navel ring jocund
Dispel
Silhouette sable
A romantic trespass
To unravel marvel
Of ballet ruffle
With glib glide gait
Navel gyrate
Will titrate
Alchemy in unfolding
Of petals' rouleau,
A smiling rose bud
On your enigmatic navel!
Coalescing sweat beads
In vermillion of setting sun

Psychedelic color play
In sparkling diamond
Butterflies zoom out
Heart sweetening
Dance on arc of rainbow
Voluptuously flummox me.
My tryst with destiny
Your enigmatic navel
My noetic ride in
Ebullient tunnel!
In sensuous navel
Bedeck floral travel
Babble twaddle tattle
Oho hoo-oo oho hoo-oo
La-la-ooh La-la-ooh
Why not join you too?

"O Woman, I am Amah and you are Saa I am Saman and you are Rik and I am sun and you earth. Let both of us unite together and procreate progeny. (Atharva Veda 14.2.71)

DAME DIVA OF GRAND VULVA

Do you know me?
In my squinting glance
I sense your presence
Around holy bushfire
In its syrupy opulence

Ooh-la-la
I am voodooed
By your magic spell
Hooked n wooed
Spewing vulva fragrance
Why I'm in brazen trance?
.

Intolerably turbulent
Am I sperming opulent
For a penny in my ouch pouch
Decored with butterfly brooch
Ah come my dear lover
Come snip my triangle top
Tear its flesh enclosure
Foliate my love deck
Satiate membrane inner
Just a zippy smooch
For my pleasure pouch
I'm juicing inside out
For your ooh-aah hug bout
I'm cathartic crush crunch
Buxom blazing brunch
Be sure to douse n drench
Make me your munch wench

Why don't you Google me?
I am on Yahoo Messenger
Cuddle dude goldie finger
Come bask in my sonsie
Trigger my areolae
Atop my love cupola
Dip your itching finger
Heave my alpha omega
Douse fire in my vulva
Navigate your utopia
Along petals of labia
Zeroing all dystopia.

"Her sexual organ is the sacrificial pit, the hair around it is the grass, her skin the soma press, the labia are the fire in middle. He who performs intercourse knowing this obtains merits of performing Vajapeya sacrifice. He who practices intercourse knowing this secures for himself the merits of the woman's good deeds, while who indulges in intercourse without knowing this passes on his own merits to the woman." (Brihad 6.4.3)

WHO WANTS MY MENSTRUATION BLOOD

I am bleeding
Yes my heart
My holes
My eyes
And if I don't bleed
What sex will I be in lead?
If I don't bleed
My heart with no compassion
What human am I?
If I don't bleed
My eyes never red with grief
What soul am I?
I bleed
To create
My son
The universe
The motherhoods
They bleed to infants bring
It is in the blood
It is in the red
Or is it in the pain
Creation all soiled with blood
And blood the look of it
All reddy, vomiting from the womb
With no warning signs
Just as it pleases
The ocean of blood
Little by little to bring an infant
It clots into a cloth bag
To softly massage the spermovamed spot
Inch by inch to snowball it

Into limbs and head and heart
And lungs and eyes and nose
The names so called
Oh the periods
Hell in the stomachs
Pain in the puberty
Agony of a mother
Sorrow of a shelterless woman
Tragedy of divine births
We bleed to create
We create in blood
Mammals we mammals
We white blooded suckle
And red blooded pickle
In pain, in blood all life
All births constrained to knife.

"When monthly illness seizes a wife, she should for three days not drink from a metal vessel, nor wear a fresh dress. Let no Shudra man or woman touch her. At the end of three days, when she has bathed, the husband should make her pound rice." (Brihad. 6.4.13)

"It is harmful for a husband to have **sex** with his wife while she is having her menses, therefore keep away from women during menses and go not unto them till they are purified. When they have purified themselves, then go in unto them as Allah has ordained for you." (سورة البقرة, Al-Baqara 2.222)

"A woman during her monthly courses, a woman who has been lately confined, and a fat woman should not be made to act the part of man during love making." (Kama Sutra)

LEANING TOWER OF PISSAH

Boiled egg white face
Curly cloudy indocile hair
Deer spry eyes
Hellenic nose
Steeping neck
Pisa's Leaning Tower
With a ruby dot
Brewing love hot
Sliced watermelon leafy lips
Ivory leggy the Dame!
Streamlet of blue blood
Flowing up visibly
From bosom
Liquid fire
On nude neck
Beguiling!
Many dived
In bosoms to die
To dye in blue beauty
Poison blue
Like tempest
Boisterous Beau
Flower Krishnachura
Glowing breathing
Fire flame singing adieu
Bon voyage to Beau?
Those blued fire
Entice, lure
Coy Decoy Beau
Impulsively enjoy
Dying in steeping neck

Bohemian bosom
Fire flames burping
Beau engages in Dame's
Ruby dot draw
Lip mark slick silken.

.

Leaning tower now says,
'Hey Dame enter in you
With body mind cargo
Guard your corpus
By angles of Euclid
Fragmented blue miniscule
With a smile face wear'.
For blue beauty poison
Muscle spasm tension
Adieu vanguards
Flag at half mast
In angled erection.

"He who inhabits the organ of generation but is within it, whom the organ does not know, whose body is the organ, and who controls the organ from within, is the Internal Ruler, your Immortal Self. He is never seen, but is the witness; He is never heard, but is the hearer; He is never thought, but the Thinker; He is never known, but the Knower. There is no other Witness but Him. There is no other knower, but Him. He is the Internal Ruler, your immortal Self. Everything else but Him is mortal." (Brihad 3.7.23)

COITUS INTERRUPTUS

Lovers they know not
blame all the men and docs
for a listless life
when one is in coma
and they do nothing

ask them to consult me
I am a woman in high street
seething in the heat
but you are a doctor
see deep into her eyes
and penetrate her seal

then there will be no surprise
yourself be not surprised
you have rendered your will
her to live in coma still

why? come and ask me
message me if you will
you are a doctor
do not let innocent ones
in coma live still
undress me and see
what lies underneath
if you have a sensible will

"Now the woman whom he desires with the thought "May she not conceive", after inserting his member in her and joining mouth to mouth, he should inhale and exhale, repeating the following mantra "With power, with semen, I reclaim the semen from you." Thus she comes to be without semen." (Brihadaranyak Upanishad 6.4.10)

BIO PSYCHIC ROMANCE

Floating silvery clouds
Vocalize vibe in me
Fragranced rummy zephyr
Flutter booze bosom
Youngish splurge spring
Ooohing nerve tentacles
Azure sky oozing smile
Concert of fragrance
Everything seems matchless
Tumultuous blood
Horripilate embrace
Why me?
Biopsychic ~ Omigod!
'Tis Lovesickness
Metastasized in fullness.
O' My Beau
I'm incurably yours
In union separation
In dilemma of Yes No
Swing de-swing of
Hope Despair.
Sitting face to face
Eyes on eyes
Souls soaked sloshed
Rill romance minstrel
Overflowing silent tryst
Under canopy cajole
Why not indulge in lofty leisure?

"In that fire Gods pour semen as their libation. From this libation arises fetus." (Chandogya Upanishad 5.8.2)

MY INNER SLUSH

Facing infinite sky
Wreathing garland
On your seductress lap
For whom knows who?
Inebriating zephyr
Brings mellow music
To gaga gala gaze why?
Love's mesmeric Mudra
Is it fugacious virtual
Or redundant real unveil
Why not now O' You?
Twilight twinkling stars
Honeying candying me
Time to be in unison dialogue
Can't listen O' You?
Why swing my bosom
By your breezy glance
Those fluffy taps pat dab
Shudder my all being
Woman of nimble spree
Your euphonic fingers'
Wreathing garland
Bedecking billowing
Of seductress lap
Park in my tote trove

"Let the two Ashvins churn the womb with two golden arani sticks! I am placing a seed in your womb to be delivered in the tenth month. As earth has fire in its womb, as heaven is pregnant with the sun, as the quarters are impregnated by air, so I am impregnating you by placing this seed in your womb." (Brihad 6.4.22)

HOLY MILK

Cyclic weeping
Overdue love flowing
Thro' virgin breast
O' Holy Milk
Who made it happen
Fracturing fragrance of trust?
O' Woman of Plenty
Punishment for sin
Dwarfing forgiveness
Given now why?
O' breast feel jamboree
Nip inertia embarrassment
From gentle sloping breast
Deliver deathless love hope
Share him hear
Vouched euphonic motherhood
Spilling relentlessly!
Ooohing! Aaaahing
Mate mansion for
Beau's face
In sousing tear
Assign you dear
Unborn to honour
As riches from love
Not lurid lust.

"O Sarasvati, that breast of thine which is stored with results, is the generous sustainer of all, full of milk, the obtainer of wealth and one's desserts, and through which thou nourishest all who are worthy of it, transfer that here to my wife to suck." (Brihad. 6.4.27)

FLESH ABSORBER

O boorish phalluses
why ne'er diverge
like ramjets crazily
on freedom's sky
why always converge
on my labial walls
all your energies
in hush push
blitch blotch
mock drills
Is my vagina
your shock absorber
for your androgen
adrenal
urge-surge
Am I to liquid sponge
Your sperm splurge?

"Woman, O Gautama, is the sacrificial fire; of that the middle part is the fuel, the hair is the smoke, the vagina is the flame, penetration is the coals and the pleasure its sparks." (Chandogya Upanishad 5.8.1)

LUXURY LINGERIE

Stealth watcher
Of XX and XY's
Vices, virtues, foreclosure
Of clandestine inclinations
Surfing incognito browser
Definer of body contours
Inspirer of personality
Share your cosy comfort
Of dame's curves and lines
Shield our bash of agony
Blush of ecstasy
Mute sensor
Of sexuality, sensuality
Sanitizer of conduct
How not to do it?
How to do it?
Almanac for our
Ethos and pathos
Sensitive gadget
Of trepidations and temptations
Peaky bosoms
Butt cleaves lissom
Of feminine cat walker
And macho pectorals
For paparazzo lens hunting
In pageantry fest
Lingerie is the sentinel
In Yin's affairs
Of bosoms' wavy ripples
Subtle musical saltation
Below bikini line

Inner thing is the scout
In Yang's crush
Fluttering above
Below the belt line
During exuberant
Romantic togetherness
Inners vicariously view
The climax glowing
Orgasms in the corpus
Of Yin, Yang
Bang bang bang

Scrap Lingerie
Deport in vat
To their lusty tryst
In romantic reminiscence
Play game of bromance
In criss-cross synergy
With others' innards
Wheeling back into
Arche romance
Of Eve and Adam
We can befool us
And some others
But not to LINGERIE
Our vigilant gizmo
Womb to tomb
Virtual reality
In amniotic sac
To cremation ash relic
Redolently hugging
Your thongs still…

MAKE ME YOUR ME

Your love
May I club
Ah your love
My decor blurb
In my pubic hub
Feelings echoing
Fill my luv tub
With your lather blob
Effulgently spilling
Over
Say
Hey
Oi
Oy
Love me why?
Tie me why?
I'm itsy-bitsy
I'm itty-bitty
I'm wee
Puncture me
Make me your me
Plant your seed
In me only
If so
I'll say okey-dokey!

"Prajapati thought 'Let me create a space where Man can establish himself'. So he created woman. He placed her sexual organ on the lower side. Therefore one should perform services on a woman on the lower side. He stretched out of himself a projectile with pleasure. With that he impregnated her.' (Brihad 6.4.2)

POLY LOVE

Whose seed it was
Of the first one
Or the second
I do not remember
Eggs mixed in saliva
Had no marker

We slid on the boat
When wind was high
I slipped into water
And he waited
And waited
On the banks
Till sun went down

A fisherman fished me
And fed me rice
I was in his cottage
For seven months

In the tenth month
I delivered a baby
I had to find a father
Baby needed a name
It was all in the game
Now I think of it
What shame.

"Soma received you first, Gandharva received afterwards. Agni became
your third husband, son of man is your fourth." (Rig Veda 10.85.40)

LOVE INSPIRING WOMEN

What men desire most
and mostly all the time
men chase women
not for only admiration

they want to find
what is hidden
beneath the silken coverage
O what a shine....
a diamond concealed
in a flourishing gold mine
sublime

will it make his love entwine
and then the two will shine
like a necklace
embedded with an emerald
in the annals of time
superfine

leaving human memory behind
the progeny we leave
is only yours
coupled with mine

"And indeed she did desire him, and he would have inclined to her desire,
had he not seen the evidence of his Lord. Thus it was, that we might turn
away from him evil and illegal **sex**ual intercourse. Surely, he was one of
Our chosen slaves." (سورة يوسف, Yusuf 12.24)

LOVE KEY HOLE

Lust love and thirst or thrust
All above are but a natural outcome
of human sexual deliberations

tell me why love
if you have no lust
also tell me why lust
if you have no love

the world revolves
about the central pole
Universal man
is in search of the key hole

all who talk about sin as such
are not human in as much
as they are all hypocrites

Tell me how will you
produce a progeny
if you have no lust
nor love of human sex

you must totally be
of a mind bereft

sad to be so blunt
and brute
now don't brood

you enforced me to be
nakedly
so blatantly rude....
yet I ain't so crude!

"Her fingers are not too smooth to handle a shovel, nor too calloused to hold thread." (Proverbs 31.16,19)

"Satan threatens you with poverty and orders you to commit sins and illegal **sex**ual intercourse; whereas Allah promises you Forgiveness from Himself and Bounty, and Allah is All-Sufficient for His creatures' needs, All-Knower." (سورة البقرة, Al-Baqara 2.268)

LOVE'S EXPIRY

Everything has expiry date
Medicine ~ Polypacked Blood
Transfusion Kit ~ Transfusion Fluid
Disposable Syringe
Male / Female ~ Contraceptives
i-Pills and IUDs
Everything has
Best use before
Pizza ~ Perfume
Lip Gloss ~ Toiletries
Sanitary napkins
Condoms – male and female
Why no expiry dates
Of Birth ~ Abortion
Life ~ Death, Love ~ Hate
Ecstasy ~ Agony
Wedding ~ Divorce
Celibacy ~ Libertinism
Sexitation ~ Frigidity
Fidelity ~ Infidelity
Virtue and Vice
Never ending culmination
Ever going contemplation.
Why no Expire Date?
Why O why?
Excogitating: $E = mc^2$?
Knows who?

When will expire
Love too?

"Then He made his offspring from semen of contaminated water of male and female **sex**ual discharge." (سورة السجدة, As-Sajda 32.8)

IN BETWEEN CHANGE

(18 Word Poetry Challenge)

Girlfriend
Changing
Dress
Before
Boyfriend.

She
Asked
Glowingly,

'In
Which
One
Looked
Best? '

Boyfriend
Quipped,

"In
Between

Change."

"Allah wishes to lighten the burden for you; and man was created weak to leave **sex**ual intercourse with woman)." (سورة النساء, An-Nisaa 4.28)

FREUD IN LOVE

pretty poem
when i read Freud
I also had a young gal
whom I'd loved
but she was only
4 years younger to me
she wanted a rich guy
married in a hurry
he flew with her
and met with
an accident

she widowed early
I do not know now
where she lives
or is
buried
but I still
love her stilled

lonely she must be
without me
I wasn't that rich
not even a cycle
I had with me

O Freud
Freud O Freud
where are you

PART SECOND

I pity Freud
he had said....
Long ones
in dreams
equal
penis...
but he never mentioned >>>>>>> ! ! !
how longggg
the sky would need...

condoms did you say?

I meant

condos
any way

"If a man desires his wife with the thought "May she enjoy love with me",
then after inserting his member inside her, joining mouth to mouth and
stroking her organ, he should utter the following mantra "O semen, you
have been produced from my every limb, especially from my heart through
the essence of the food. Bring this woman under my control like a deer
pierced by a poisoned arrow." (Brihadaranyak Upanishad 6.4.9)

EUNUCH LOVE

They were gyrating
under their skirts
like frogs in motion

love chugged along
on limping legs
belching out smoke

square finger tips
drew blank lines
on tattooed cheeks

a smoking gun
belched out a kiss
from dry vacant lips

thick rainless clouds
dropped hot winds
on smokeless pyres

Smell of burnt ghee
Of sacrificial fire
In shallow armpits

From the sweat drops
of their nascent love
a nymph was born

"When the organ of generation went out of the body, we lived just like eunuchs, without producing children through our organs of generation, but lived through the vital force." (Brihad 6.1.12)

COME RAPE ME

Poetry rolls forward: -
Come on rape me
With prurient plunge
Sense the stinging
Embracing warmth
Of gamma ray
My females
Are programmed
To emasculate
Radioactively
An exemplary
Resort needed
To dodo rapists.

"If she is not willing, he should buy her over; and if she is still unyielding, he should strike her with a stick or with the hand and proceed, uttering the following Mantra, 'I take away your reputation,' etc. She is then actually discredited. (Brihadaranyak Upanishad 6.4.7)

"Flee from sexual immorality. All other sins a person commits are outside the body, but whoever sins sexually, sins against their own body."
(Corinthians 6:18)

PART - II

AN EYEFUL OF LUST

EYES SEE NOT
WHEN MIND IS BLIND

AND A BABY IS BORN

Truth is naked. Truth was, is and will ever be. But we humans like to wear masks.

To perceive pure love that is God, you have to unmask your heart, unmask your soul, unmask the purity of your being.

Mind, reasoning and all sensory knowledge are only stumbling blocks in realising the pure purity of being. When you realise this simple truth, you give up all thinking. And when you give up thinking the ugly clothing will fall down. The naked cabaret dancer will start dancing. Beauty will flow, hearts will smile, penetrating your being with knives and organs made of pure energy. Then a little baby you will become. Like amoeba, you are the mother, you are the kid.

LUSTY LOVER

It is more of lust
behold
yes it must be cold
you need someone to hold
in bed
as per your desire
you just said
as you lay alone
hoping she would come for you

and

do all that you wish her to do
yes when alone
when you are done
you may say well done

come again
when I am alone

in my imagination
come lets now change
from lust to love
leaving out that imaginary
handful of frustration....
come
love, come

"But I tell you that if you look at another woman and want her, you are
already unfaithful in your thoughts." (**Matthew 5:28**)

TIPSY EYES AND CRIMSON THIGHS

Are you the naked Earth
with gravity in your Centre
attracting me and mine
with unlimited wonder

Do you have magnets
fixed at your breast ends
every time you pass by
pivoted they signals send

are the tenders in your laps
nectar buds of crimson thighs
drunken hips and tipsy eyes
simply winking me and mine

have you birds' cooing
from the belly domes
they shake me up
and skate me down

I shudder at the idea
of the fertile soil within
your raining landscape
in poisonous shapes.

"For everything in the world—the lust of the flesh, the lust of the eyes, and the pride of life—comes not from the Father but from the world." (**John 2:16)**

BEAUTY IN THE THIGHS

If beauty could be revealed
just by showing a thigh
guys would come flying by
then don't feel shy
they will lift you sky high
and see
what more lies beneath the sky
all along your thigh

as you smile and wish
many more guys
will come by
to wrap about your soft thigh
one by
as they fling you off
you would ask for more
you simply showed just a thigh
O why

They'll ask why
then don't then be shy
do not cry
guys will continue to pry
then you won't be able to deny
show them your other thigh !!
But don't ask me why

"When the woman saw that the tree was good for food, and that it was a delight to the eyes, and that the tree was desirable to make one wise, she took from its fruit and ate; and she gave also to her husband with her, and he ate." (Genesis 3:6)

WOMAN'S NAKED TRUTHS

A naked woman
is a sight to see
when her breasts
are free to eyes
till your mind
tricks your find
and the body
turns your wife and mother
when your daughter
peeps from the height
and urges you
to look at the sight
Fatherhood oh, Fatherhood
you stumbled upon
naked truth
and that is life
that is anybody's life.

"I have made a covenant with my eyes; How then could I gaze at a virgin?
(Job 31-1)

PICTURE OF PLUNGING TRIPS

Heart of a maid
hips of lovely strides
snaking our thoughts
the breasts
the thighs
the plunging trips
they are the pictures
of your youth
kindling the desire to mate
and senses to consummate
dont give up
dont give up
it is simply the song of life
music lingers on long
after the end of desire
go now smoke your pipe.

"Tell the believing men to lower their gaze from forbidden things, and protect their private parts from illegal **sex**ual acts. That is purer for them. Verily, Allah is All-Aware of what they do." (سورة النور, An-Noor 24.30)

BEAUTY OF CURVES

the flash of youth
the glaze of cheeks
the gleam in those looks
the wine in those words

I found beauty of the curves
in the moons and waves of blue
then in the hips and lips
and clueless horizons
haunting the tips

the coal black curls
the queenly strides
the mesmeric motions
and the hypnotising emotions

when life bubbled
surfaced everything so sweet
and when the winds reversed
the holed lungs battered

Butterfly beings
Dew like doings
Cloudy existence
Deserted all sense.

"Charm is deceitful, and beauty is vain, but a woman who fears the Lord
is to be praised." (Proverbs 31.30)

NAKED ME WITHIN

Undress me
unto my death
naked I shall bear
generations to fear

Uncover me
I shall shiver with passions
to litter piglets of rations
to eat faecal matters.

Unveil me
my emotions bared
Mirror my heart
to see me part by part

to observe my reactions
and cause behind actions
to study the impulses
and reciprocative pulses

with a knife of sharp precision
cut apart the hypocrisy in my fashion
give my hands the strength to penetrate
me myself and find out all the adulterates

Naked all of us transpire
into one universal truth
that the cloth lining was really untrue
and that we are all made of one fine hue

look me inside

wash off and wipe off
all the dirt and dust
the clean being digests not

lies and instincts of animal sorts
all ugly vulgar emotions vapourise
to bring the rainy hours of real sunrise
when facts unadulterated with fictions
throw light upon real functions

Naked thou are holy
naked you face yourself truly
yes, you are half bad, half good
that is the same as anybody on earth should.

****

"Do not desire her beauty in your heart,
Nor let her capture you with her eyelids.
For on account of a harlot one is reduced to a loaf of bread,
And an adulteress hunts for the precious life.
Can a man take fire in his bosom
And his clothes not be burned?
Or can a man walk on hot coals
And his feet not be scorched?
So is the one who goes in to his neighbor's wife;
Whoever touches her will not go unpunished. (Proverbs 6:25-29)

DAWN LOVE

like a fragile glass
dawn opens
its soft golden fur
slowly touches the greens
upon the leaves of coconut
the sweet breeze fiddles upon
little by little the warmth creeps in

like the innocent blushes
of maidens in the villages
first the east pinkens
stars of stirring passions
gently disappear
taking refuge
in the crowded sky
strange coloured cloud
and the melody melts the dew
freed from the veil of shyness
peeping out from the blues
the beauty of growing love
blossoms fill with nectar

from the nature the bees learn
flocking at the flowers in turn
birds of dawn breathing fresh
songs of heart flooding earth
new symphonies unfold depths.

"When Surya went towards her husband, the sky and earth became the
carriage, her awareness became the back cushion, and her vision became
eye make-up." (Rg Veda 10.85.7)

I WAS AWAKE ALL NIGHT

When rains whitewash the blue skies
the nights are full of sparkling stars
the sky is sown with smiling gems
like shawls of queens embedded with stones

Pure light it drips down
liquid light is a sight to delight
drops of lovely tranquility falls
and meets eyes with majestic calls

From heavens solitary serene balls
lustrous beauties slip down to looks
washed and clean and neat they gleam
as you lay awake all night on grassy streams.

Editor's Note :- Hemangi Sharma wrote it on July 26, 2015 – the day before she met in person for the first time in this life. She had spoken to me at length on that night over phone. This was one of her last poems as "Lalitha Iyer".)

"It is lawful for you to have **sex**ual relations with your wives on the night of As-Saum fasting. They are your body cover and you are the same for them. Allah knows that you used to deceive yourselves. He forgave you. So now have **sex**ual relations with them and seek that which Allah has ordained for you. Eat and drink until the white thread of dawn appears to you distinct from the black thread of night, then complete your fasting till nightfall. Don't have **sex**ual relations with your women while you are in the mosque for prayers. These are the limits set by Allah, so that you become pious." (سورة البقرة, Al-Baqara 2.187)

I WATCH THE CLOUDS FLY AWAY

As I lie upon my couch
I could watch the flying pouches
silky breasts milky rich
like fantasy they glide beyond reach

As they swam across in haste
I feel as if my globe is being chased
wind carrying them far off
as if time is flying into ages dug

It is a beauty to watch them pass by
as if they are participants of some race
galaxies run with laughing clouds
galloping in horses with delicate moulds

They are my youth and dreams and passions
before I could figure out, they have passed away
lingering heart could not make out them properly
but they have vanished into uncertainty land

I turn my time machine and peep into my past
life flows away as we try to understand the truths
as we attempt to balance inner and outer worlds
and weigh each and every being with meaning

and before we could even decide
we are forced to commitments unseeing.

"For all that is in the world, the lust of flesh and lust of eyes and the boastful
pride of life, is not from the Father, but is from the world." (John 2.16)

LOVE WITH THE BLUE

Blue sky deep
washed by rains
stand out drained
All colours swept off
only blue escaped the wipe

snow white clouds
cotton balling in the sky
ice cream moulds
sailing high
dreams of white
galloping at night
its a sight to see
the wandering clouds

stars, shining bright
veiled beneath
like beautiful girls
smile sweetly
hidden discreetly
beneath the bulging softness
they delight us
just coyly blinking

As I lie upon the grass
and watch the night sky
my senses rich and fertile
devoid of fatigue the day piled
dissolving into night's delights
after the rains pure azure sky

Divine mother she caves in
all my senses she covers
I absorbed into her vanities
and melt into a timeless symphony

Clouds their grey breasts relieved
the milk of life suckled by earth
sailing to other end of globe
carried by whispering breeze
with a drunken intoxication
where are they going and why
are they purely physical or heavenly
stars are they physical or heavenly
who created clouds and who me?
so lovely are they, yet why
they do not speak to me
why do I fall in love with them
yet, they don't
what is more in a star,
that I don't have
what is more in me
that a star does not have
The clouds pass by leaving behind questions new
already I am a waste bin of thoughts
every new life appears before me
heaps the waste of ideas in me
with the touch of every being
I am crowded with cloudy feelings.

"Be soft gazed, not a husband slayer, benefactor of animals, pleasant hearted, bright looking, mother of heroes, devoted to God. Be peaceable with all men and animals." (Rg Veda 10.85.44)

WET SUNSET

Everything is wet
when the sun sets
sea shores
soiled feet
salty sand
and silent tears

When dusk nears
heart beats shiver
something whispers
and sadness spreads

It is an odd hour
clasping hands tremor
kissing lips unsure
lusty passions wear
it's a time of mystery
of earth and the sea
and the raging ocean
across the beds of crests
ruthless beats her breast
something is let loose
when the sun sets
my erotic confusions
and aimless fears
drown me into misty layers
I just look into the horizon
and watch the burning graves
father, mother and loved ones dear
painted across the evening sky

PART – III

SOUNDS OF LOVE

WHISPERS FROM ETERNITY

TALKING WITH GOD

God knows the thoughts of our hearts before they land on our tongues. One who tunes into God knows the thoughts welling up in all human hearts. One who loves God knows how to talk to God in silence.

For wherever life is, there is talking. Talking is a beauty of life link, of being in existence. Talk of feelings, talk of emotions, talk of not only words but heavenly responses to nature, wind, breeze, ocean, sky, birds and all. In silence body talks, in darkness inner light talks. At night the nocturnals talk. In peace hearts talk with love. In harmony music talks with symphonies. Talking without words is the most beautiful talking. Talking with dance, talking with lyrics, talking with memories, nostalgic. When you are old and alone, you will talk to photos of dead ones, to tombs of dead ones, to your beloved ones gone by. You talk to your own feelings, you talk to them who are in your consciousness. Talking is as enormous as your silent gifts of love.

Talk to God. Talk with your heart absorbed in God. Listen incessantly to God's silent talk. Do not underestimate the power of the Word. And do not forget that the pen is mightier than all the injustices that holy earth can contain. Writing is a source of personal soul-searching to find the meaning of life on earth.

For when God's light opens my heart, I hear the laughter of innocence in my being.

THE MATING CALL

The mating call
of the male Cuckoo
it is so disturbing
that you feel like
going up to the tree
and softly caress the bird

It melts your heart
touches you deep within
for ages it is the same
the urge is persistent
and compels you
to respond in love

The passion is very strong
burning all inhibitions
diving into velvety depths
of the female's heart
and hypnotizing her
with mellowed plea
you can't refuse the call
neither can you ignore
it goes straight like an arrow
and knows its way like a shot
tempting with eloquence
and tempted
from lands apart

"If she give in, he says: "With manly strength and glory I give thee glory,"—
and thus they both become glorious." (Brihad 6.4.8)

A SINGLE MELODY

You and I,
we sang like little nightingales
You sang, I sang
We shared sweet little smiles
You were the lips, I was the smile

In times of tears
You held me close to you
You wiped my tears
I held your hand

You were the flesh, I was the skin
The golden sun smiled,
you were the gold, I was the light

You hugged me, I caressed you
You were the fingers, I was the body

When the songbird sang in our hearts
You were one wing, I was the other wing

We were two candles but one flame
I was the sparkling sea,
You were the ripples
You sing, I sing
We are a single melody.

"He embraces her saying, 'I am the vital force, and you are speech; you are speech, and I am the vital force ; I am Saman, and you are Rc;I am heaven, and you are the earth; come, let us strive together so that we may have a male child." (Brihadaranyak Upanishad 6.4.20)

YOUR FLUTE PLAYED ON ME

O beloved sweetheart
melodies of your flute
have stolen my heart

When your love tunes
reached my waiting ears
I lost consciousness
I felt I lost my body

Was I in a trance??

I saw your love flute
playing melodious tunes
of rippling romance
on my body dunes

And on my love bed
I was mesmerized
and then transfixed
by your dream gaze.

"He should then seat her on his left side, and holding her hair, and also touching the knot of her garment, he should gently embrace her with his right arm. They may the sing, either with or without gesticulation, and play on various musical instruments…." (Kama Sutra)

TOUCH ME WITH A HARP

You touched me
with a hand
oh no, with a harp
with the cool air
of your silent love
kissing the strings
setting them to songs
of mountain springs
you touch me now
with a lyric of desire
a soft music
a song in melody
that is love
the music of life
the singing voice of living
is love, silently aloud
the more quiet
the air is
the more fuller the feel is
when smiles condense
into single tears
to fall or not to fall
becomes an uncertainty
as they collect near the ends
and bulge into drops
inner beauty shines
in the looks of desire
drained into tear drops
all lamps of the holy lit
into the ponds bright
as it dawns

the stars of puzzles
they walk off
no more questions
all answers are sunned
radiant is the mind
the heart - a houseful board
no more entries
memories sentries
they weave and web
of little wonders hub.

"When you follow the desires of your sinful nature, the results are very clear: sexual immorality, impurity, lustful pleasures, idolatry, sorcery, hostility, quarreling, jealousy, outbursts of anger, selfish ambition, dissension, division, envy, drunkenness, wild parties, and other sins like these. Let me tell you again, as I have before, that anyone living that sort of life will not inherit the Kingdom of God." (**Galatians 5:19-21**)

CUCKOO'S CALL

It calls
Cooes I recall
when I was a child
it was very mild
as my teens grew
I leaned against its flow
why the Cuckoo calls
my son asks,
as I peep from window falls

Why the heart breaks
when the decibels seek
with earnest desire to find
some mate of similar bind
the poor bird
striving blind
as if it plunges the knife
into the unanswering wife

the trail of the long tune
missiling from the wretched groom
when the winter nights close up
and air begins to dry up
emotionally parched thoughts sprout out
the spongy hearts spiky mouthed
aches begin to find a mate

wherever you are
whoever you be
when the Cuckoo calls
it bakes the very walls

of sleeping palls
when it cooes
it pours out woes
of yours and mine
who is without thine...

the call is clear
truth and honest
unlike human lust
the bird needles the breast
of every lovelorn bust
tearing apart the freezing apathy
of empty world without sympathy
it cooes and cooes till the mate appears
inducing form into the empty airs
transforming the tangential branch
into a haven of multiple switch....

"When the man strike the woman's head with the fingers of his hand, the appropriate sounds are the cooing sound, and the sounds Phat and Phut. At the end of congress, the sighing and weeping sounds are made." (Kama Sutra)

"But I discipline my body and make it my slave, so that, after I have preached to others, I myself will not be disqualified." (Corinthians 9.27)

GAME OF SONGS

Standing you are
On the opposite bank
Of my soul song

Ambulant my tunes
Become Me
Don't get you
Breeze is blowing
Oh, oh excellently
Keep anchored the boat
No more.

Cross and come, O Dear
Into my bosom's abode
Game of songs with you
Game of distance is
Me in agony play flute
All the time

When O Dear
Yourself will come
Take my flute to play

In the dense darkness of
Rapture-full silent night.

"When excited during love, a woman continually utters words expressive of prohibition or desire of liberation, as well as words like 'father', 'mother' intermingled with sighing, weeping and thundering sounds. Towards conclusion, her body should be pressed with palm, and sounds of quail or goose should be made." (Kama Sutra)

SOFT WHISPERS OF LOVE

Softly they whisper
the hearts of love
tenderly they kiss
the hour of dove.

they are not starry headed
they are blind hearts
they are not moony bedded
they are life blooded

they are found in the grassy beds
in the lap of tiny dew-wet lawns
in the squirrels lusty leaps
in the pigeons velvety neck to neck pecks.

when I lie upon the night
in the sandy shores
they sail across the smelling waves
and caress my locks lulling my eyes

they are not bought and sold in shops
they are not luminaries in the pops
they are not commercial heroines or heroes
they are just lovely heavenly bliss hidden inside shoes

they cup inside the fragrant flowers
they coo with the winter birds
they lick you like the pet puppy wild
they give love with a heart of purest child.

when the magic wand is on
all leaves turn into viola strings
all trees guitarists hands
and all air vibrant with mysterious sounds.

when the lazy earth seeded with passions sperm
longs to sleep in lethargic icy costumes
babes of beauty they crawl and climb
upon my heart with hugs and lisping rhymes.

"When a woman's body is struck with one's palm during love making, she utters various hissing sounds, and also eight types of crying – such as the sound hin-hin, thundering sounds, sound of cooing, weeping, Phut, Phat, Sut and Plat…." (Kama Sutra)

"Dear friends, I warn you as 'temporary residents and foreigners' to keep away from worldly desires that wage war against your very souls." (**Peter 2:11**)

I HEAR THE MONSOON'S KNOCK

Monsoon brings in cool rains
colour of earth in lovely paints
it is true that monsoon rains heal
all the wounds that summer peals

What odd transformations
with rain rains new passions
strange emotions, stranger illusions
silly lusts and stupid profusions.

Rain Queen arrives later
first comes the whistling wind
pregnant with moist love
the winds dance around every country leaf

she does not arrive quiet
the air metamorphosed into some delicate night
day is singing with luxurious feelings
sun to rains, the heart claps and mind flutters wings.

If the air is so beautiful before she comes
if the message is so sweet in itself
if the engagement is in Paradise
if the window opened is full of light
how could I describe the Monsoon delight?

When you hear the knock at green door steps
tip-tap, sip-sap, softly, gently and then paces
the lovely embrace tightens its grips
whispers loudly start announcing
and it is clear, she is sure to descend

the rains blending and bleaching pure
earth with muddy paint
and nature with flawless taint.

Music she brings pop and popular
it pitches high and low, hard and fast
rhythmic drops they patter upon rooves
designing forms upon the ground
and deeply ponding every country mount

I am speechless, reactions statued
expressions solidified to wax perplexions
to what lofty heavens did she lift me
to what paradise did she transfer mine's

Music is not what ear hears
music is not just what harmonious sound weaves
music is finding a rhythm in life
some meaning when the heart opens out
some sudden hand from deepest caves

Something connects you to some inner in-thing
some delightful meaning for your existence
you find the cord, all discords melting imminently
some clue, oh no, it is an answer to the ageless torment

Music sweep away and here vanishes the gap of imprisoned
the cage is broken open, the bird is free in glee
Music is in the sound of branches and trees
birds chirp and clouds burp
but rain's music fills me completely divined.

A LEAF WHISPERS ON MY BODY TREE

Little little whispers
from tiny tiny leaves
they rustle among trees
or in the dust heaps
Yet, touch my heart to weep.

Green and red,
gorgeously veined,
yellow leaves with holy aches
when I stand near the trees
they quiver in my inner deeps
pulling my insides out.

When I watch them vibrate swift
They swirl around in every lovely graze
Slow and fast, tempestuous and cozily,
Fanned by hot mid air
They wave to me things infinite.

I am stunned
to watch the amazing varieties;
tiny, big, velvety, artistic,
Chiseled carvings in supple greens
Watch out countless are the species;
Every leaf of nature is our teacher
Cooks of nature, food and finest cosmic features
Every leaf has a history,
A story in its heart
And a legend in its silky breast.

my life's gloom cool

I dance like a puppet girl.
the leaves are lovely, plenty, vivid
full of imaginations of my childhood views.
They flash and flash in more of blazing beauty
of life, passions, lust and emotions, volatile.

Leafless trees with nests of birds
reminds me of those Spring days
when leaves used to cuddle branches
Coconut leaves like guitar strings
Banana leaf like Noah's Arc
pregnant with tradition's tale and their aroma
The boat shaped beauty
such huge womb, like a mother's
with a homely flavor and hugging air

lovely banyan hearts
reflecting heavenly mansions of throbs
some leaves shiver with trembles within me
they shake in the air with such gentle rapidity
that I feel the charge of nature within my spine
every leaf zooms into my mind's panorama
and every single wing it spreads
with snuggling furs

I relish, it is an eternal pleasure.

"When a woman, placing one of her feet on her lover's foot, and the other
foot on his thighs, passes one of her arms around his back and the other
one on his shoulders, making the sound of cooing and singing, and wishes
as if to climb up him to plant a kiss, it is called an embrace like climbing of
a tree'". (Kama Sutra)

VIRGIN SONG OF UNSEENS

A virgin
for one
you can tell
when you meet first
an idea
if original
the first line
itself spells
that the verses
are not curses
like the fresh Spring
her flowers in strings
virgin beauty pops up
as words speak up
when you touch the middle
you feel the choice a riddle
but when you end
there is the find
the heart lies there
a tiny woven bundle
you begin
and you are doubtful
you don't know
how much you missed
when you just kissed
you first want to finish
the whole thing fast
then again you fish
for things you missed
again you recount
what was the first thing

where did the line bring
the act with the image link
how the theme suited
with the music setted
oozing with richness
the fertile sounds fence
words of life and hence
we sit brooding all day
the marvel blend of ways
every part of it
as you begin instead
sounds as a separate kit
spelling the sweet mint
her fragrance
fresh from the garden of Eden
her skin aching to taste
the magic of the mission
every word a world of suction
we touch the book
the page, the strip
and lost are we adrift
hugging close
losing self in loose
moods of ageless forms
dance within the arms
urging to read more
to learn the untold lore
to discover, where the poet uncovered not
to peep into his unseens
shared verses
and sentenced muses
kindle the urge to seek
more treasures in his reek.

SOUND OF THOUGHT

Have you ever heard
the sound of thoughts
a pebble of word
dropped in Silence
as the eyes speak
and looks write in eloquence
have you ever felt
your fingertips itch to ink
the ideas oozing from pinks
the message from hearts
in the language of emotions
when Great men think
connecting many links
could you understand
why the way they shrink
with multitudes in wink

got any idea
about my study area
it is the sound of the vowels
emerging from the levels
where You and I cant revel
when I say aloud
you say it is the language sound
of English, German or French counts
you can write meanings from dic down
how can you measure
when at leisure
the airing of thoughts
without a syllable apart
I speak in Silence

you talk with breath
with your inner lips
many a divine men of Order
spoke with unwritten tongues
you understood without ears
and language books

Every being sends messages
a tree, a sparrow, rain and thunder shower
I am serious, just listen to me clear
every matter emanates symbols
signs of secrecies
they tell everybody things
clues about their livings
and as you shut up more and more
you can listen to voices sure
as you pass people in the city
in the villages and valleys
they speak in futile
creating noises unfertiles
in Silence, the music of life
templed in all matters wise

I am too lengthy,
sorry, my muse is more strengthy
do u hear dear
when all are silent
they speak more talent
the inner talk is eternal
it goes on and on
the Voice of thought is on
and our moods and minds
are only gifts of flooding binds.

PART – IV

TOUCH OF WILD

SECRETS OF SENSUALITY

LOVE ALONE

The whole life is a search for a little bit of love. If we do not get it, we become psychologically and physically ill. If we experience it, then there is Rhythm in our souls and we dance in those rhythms...

All the moments in which you do not love, are wasted moments of life which will never come back. Our call is to love. There is no meaning in life without love.

Love and love alone can bring you into the world of beauty. Your soul is in need of love. The deepest longing in you is love. Love is spiritual nourishment.

Love is God's hands and arms. He hugs his beings through love. When we are pure in mind, or when there is no mind, God puts his hand made of divine energy through our hearts. Through us that hand goes to the heart of our beloved. Now who are you, and who am I, to stop, start, punctuate, and intervene that love?

I GAVE HIM MY BODY

I was young
He loved me well
I gave my body
flesh all fresh

the breasts were lovely
the thighs were sweet
everything was
enough for a treat

I thought he loved me
he needed me
for the lovely shapes

I needed him
he was a man to take
me along the lands unknown
and give me a hand
when the unsure mind stemmed

When young a man's desire is painted clear
but, wonder what the maid seeks
but for her folly, nothing at all he speaks

his words are not wisdom
his acts are not kingly
he is as much poor
as the maid to his core

she bears better weight
and really faces the tight

when she kisses
not him, but delivery stresses

She brings the babies
gives them sweetness
and when she cries
she teaches them wisdom
when she failed to pass her own

Now, when he is past prime
I have nothing to spare
if he something ask dare

my body is realised
my mind fully piled
what is in his love
that only strokes my flesh with filth;

let him prove his affection
by cooking my favourite collection
let him prove his love
by washing my dresses dirty
and smiling at me saintly.

"Verily, we have created man from Nutfah of mixed **sex**ual discharge of
man and woman, in order to try him: so we made him hearer and seer."
(سورة الانسان, Al-Insaan 76.2)

SUN KISS ON MY CHEEKS

The tropical sun kisses me
on both my cheeks today
as I go talking and chatting
to the flitting butterflies
on the way to my school

I feel the warmth and the cold
of dark skinned forest leaves
I hear the music of the leaves
when wind blows on them

I imagine they are all lovers,
the trees, the leaves and the wind
and I want to be the wind

flying along the shuffling leaves
and making them dance
to the undulating tunes
of my whistling breeze
and making them smile

softly with me.

"When a girl, setting aside her bashfulness a little, wishes to touch the lip
that is pressed into her mouth, and with that intention moves her lower lip,
but not the upper one, then it is called a 'throbbing kiss'." (Kama Sutra)

WOULD YOU HUG ME

When the roses wait
for the kiss of the dew,
when the first rays of the sun
touch the tiny beaks
of the singing bird
when in my soft smiling lips
and in my shining eyes
you see thousand little stars
hiding in my soul

secretly

would you hug me innocently
and give me a soft kiss
whose memory will lead me
from this glorious dawn
through to the dusk?

"When a woman, clinging to a man as a creeper twines around a tree, bends his head down with the desire of kissing him, and makes slight sounds with her mouth, embraces him, and then looks lovingly toward him, it is called an embrace like 'twining of a creeper'." (Kama Sutra)

I FELT YOU INSIDE ME

when we slept
I felt you slipping inside
my curved contours
overhead the colors raged
in pink, white and crimson
bikini clouds slyly clubbed
in grey feather formations
launching the water ladder
to slip down into heart of earth
changing forms at will
within blinks of eyes
the sacred spirits
sinked into earthen cups of mud
and slowly slept at the heart
desirous of a union so sweet
jumping from their heavenly mansions
stepping through the rainy apparitions
and smelling into the earthly passions.....

while I locked you in
curvature of my legs
secure inside me

"When two lovers lie on a bed and embrace each other so closely that the arms and thighs of one are encircled by the arms and thighs of the other, and are rubbing against them, it is called an embrace like a mixture of 'sesame seeds and rice'." (Kama Sutra)

YOU SNEAKED INTO MY HIPS

You touched me
in my dreams
I felt you like real
and let out screams
when I woke up
you were near
and then I screamed
took it for a dream

Are you near
it is not clear
as I sit you next
you look an unseen text
and when I sleep
you slip into my hips
the flavour you love
i wonder all hours
dozing off dulled by colours
in my silences
u come as fragrances
I wonder are u true
or am I untrue
when I met you
under the College gate
my words choked
and questions blocked
how could I ask
do u swim
into my lands of dreams
when during encounters
you struggle with tenders.

TOUCH MY NOOKS N CRANNIES

O eternal flame of love,
how I wait in my bridal attire
that you visit me tonight
and kindle in me
your fire of passion?

Would you blaze down tonight
on dark contours of my desires
to wound me again with love
till you reach the very roots
of my thirsting soul

Come touch me in my depths
in my secret crannies tonight
with the soft feathery touch
of your titillating warm love

Destroy my body's hunger
with the torch beam of passion
Stir in my nooks and crannies
the desire for secret love
and help me lie awake
till morning hours
in your loving embrace.

"The places which are to be pressed with nails are – the armpits, the throat, the breasts, the lips, buttocks, abdomen and the thighs. But when the heat of passion becomes excessive, time and place need not be considered."
(Kama Sutra)

VOLTAGE OF YOUR TOUCH

Blinded with lightning
of charged intensity,
the flow of electricity
heavily voltaged
sensitivity topped
You touched me
with fingers, oh no
with thoughts
provoking my inner feelings
with a thunder heart
pondering the depths
of my clueless life
glued to your looks
streaming lazer rays
full of wisdom
and cosmic truths
spilling out
like multitude of sperms
yet, my ovum
will you be able
to catch just one
to mature into
a fully shrined Buddha..

"She should take hold of her lover by the hair, bend his head down, kiss his lower lip, and intoxicated with love, should shut her eyes and bite him at several places." (Kama Sutra)

LIPS TO REJOICE

Why worry?
Mortals worry
they are not Ivory;
full of feelings and emotions
thoughts that blink
at every dangerous link,
sink at every losing brink
humans worry, dear madam
we are not angels
neither gods of elixirs
we want to inhale the moments
of life afresh
lips to kiss
and kids we miss
sex we rejoice
saintly we pray
silent we wish
like an eternal song
melody be our metre
and passion be our gesture
I dont want to be a corpse
nor my lovely mansion
be sick with killing ills.

"All the places that can be kissed are also the places that can be bitten, except the upper lip. The lower lip is the place on which 'hidden bite', 'swollen bite' and the 'pointed bite' are made." (Kama Sutra)

SWEAT OF SUN'S LUST

Sweat of the Sun
have you ever seen
it is the sweetest
or is the hottest
is it filthy
or tasting salty

Sweat of the labour
of lust and harbour
after the virginity
outgrows the cavity
and man and woman
lie waisted and wishful
does it tastes
the pain of kindled thirst

Sweat is sweetest
smell is strongest
and stretch is farthest
when it emanates
from the concentrates
of the labour
who under scorching sun
toils to feed
hungry mouths of his own deeds.

"When a man bites a woman forcibly, she shoud do the same with double
force. Thus a 'point' should be returned with a 'line of points', and a 'line
of points with a 'broken cloud'. (Kama Sutra)

MOON, BATHE ME

Love flows with perfect grace
like the dove that wants to fly.

I remember her embrace.

Hold me my desire oh my heart!

Moon, come and bathe me,
caress me.

As the feathers of a wing
cuddle together,
I want to cuddle with you
and gaze at your face
with golden light
shining in my eyes.

"May you conceive, O Moon-faced one. May you conceive, O Energy of
Creation. May the two Ashvins wreathed with lotuses, grant conception to
you." (Atharva Veda.5.25.3)

HE LOVES AND LICKS

He hugs me
kicks me too
kisses me
licks me too
enraged
when denied the stage
he too treats my cage
too little and leave me outraged

he is my son
my heart's mansion
is full of his funs
i wake up to him
sleep unto him
he fills my world
with life and hold

when sweet love touches
the touch is above matches
i am soaked with love
too much and truly cowed.

"The biting, which is done by bringing together the lips and the teeth of lovers, is called the 'coral and the jewel'. Lip is the coral and teeth the jewel." (Kama Sutra)

CURVES AND QUIVERS

A curve
in full silvery light
a full moon
a meeting of curves
an arch
the fashionable curve
a wave
the passionate weave
all beauty
in curves of heart
the dove's bosom
dodging touch by action
the lovely breasts
curving from virginity
to eternity's unrest.
milking love
and molten passions
splitting hearts
and spilling iron thoughts
all curves in hips
and lips and
she stoops
to curve me
down and down
to win her over
and win me all quivers

"The signs of enjoyment and satisfaction of the woman are as follows –
her body relaxes, she closes her eyes, she puts aside all bashfulness and
shows increasing eagerness to unite with her lover as closely as possible."
(Kama Sutra)

LOVE SAPLING ON MY BREASTS

A new lust
seeded yester night
during sleep
by hands unseen
in the fertile soil
lying within deep
all afresh
as I woke up
saplings of love
mushroomed in my breasts
softly I caressed
the lovely little things
dreams have come true
yes, poppy plants they are
intoxicating me
with luxuriant vapour

you sit in the sit-outs
and search for hands
that hug your bosom
and caress with systems
spells cast upon
spilling magic borns.

"The curved marks made with fingernails on a woman's breasts are called a 'peacock's foot'. When her lover, before going on a distant journey, makes such a mark on her thighs or her breasts, it is called a 'token of remembrance'." (Kama Sutra)

HOT CLOUDS ON WARM BREASTS

I wish
a Rain would come
yes, the heat is killing
and I am stroked by fatigue
oh, the first rain
with drops of love
just to lick my heat
off the body of lust
to fill with coolness
strawing away
with passion the sinking hotness
oh, what a sight
of grey clouds like breasts of milk
aching to pour
what a beauty
it is about to rain
let us dance and play
the dust will be wet
earth crust set
for the new seed
new sprout to shoot
cheering hearts with bouts.

"The biting of a lover on a woman's breasts, which consist of unequal risings in a circle, and which get imprinted from the space between the lover's teeth, are called 'broken clouds'. (Kama Sutra)

LET ME COOL YOUR BED

The bed in your heart
I beg to spare for me
I shall rest
as I am infest
with the wounds from life
from too much strife
to you I seek
the alms of hopes
and trust of taste
and link of lines
i shall sweep it neat
with my hair plates straight
wipe the dirts
with innocent arts
smoothen the ridges
with hands of sensing bridges
intensify the joys
by dancing with toys
lessen you sorrows
by chirping with sparrows
cool it with kisses
and calm it with wishes.

"Young people can live a clean life by obeying your word. I worship you with all my heart. Don't let me walk away from your commands." (**Psalms 119:9-10**)

TUGGING AT MY SKIRT

Though I love You
my thoughts tug at my skirts
days are numbered
dusk is setting on
they point to me
go on
don't stop
this heart wont bear
when the wave recedes
and Ocean no more tides

Though his hands
I could touch
they smell of a future
of dying mess
My dreams speak of
days to come
when life will kill me
with lonely aches

"When two lovers are walking slowly together, either in the dark, or in a place of public resort, or in a lonely place, and rub their bodies against each other, it is called 'rubbing love'. (Kama Sutra)

BATHE MY BODY IN LOVE

When his part finishes
and when he departs
I wonder how could I
bear the broken heart
Tonight his passionate hug
it permeates
into me a Season of Lust
but hidden beneath
looms largely
the hour of future
part of nature

Take me
not just my body
Wipe me off the thoughts
that trouble my days and nights
the consciousness
the killing rationality
that shakes me vigorously
take me
undress my thoughts
and bathe me with insanity
let me love and let me mate.

"When a person presses the chin, the breasts, lower lip or thighs of his lover so softly that no scratch or mark is left, but only the hair on the body become erect from that touch, and the nails pressing the body make a sound, then it is called 'sounding or pressing with nails'." (Kama Sutra)

KILLER WAVES ENTER MY HIPS

The waves
they call you
come on
come to my bed
like a lovely lass
they hug your feet
and upset your stand
your steps deter
and again the next
they wet you
and cooling rises up
slowly you are won
the message
has worked
you go more and more
nearer the deeps
you want to feel
the massive heap
and write your name
upon the wet sands
the nearer you go
the higher they climb
and enter the hips
with drugging moisture

"A horse having once attained the fifth degree of motion goes on with blind speed, regardless of pits, ditches and posts on his way; and similarly a loving pair become blind with passion in the heat of intercourse, and go on with impetuosity, paying not even the least regard to excess." (Kama Sutra)

TOUCH ME WITH YOUR HEART

Touch me
with your wild heart
with its raw emotions
flowing down like lotions
spill them every portion
on my body pores
and fill me like an Ocean
lovely little thoughts
I love to hug with spots
little ideas flashing
chasing me I enjoy
Come touch me with your Heart
your beauties are my wives
come on my beauties
I share with your Knights
your words of deeper insights
and verses of richer lights
oh, come on give me a hand
to lavish in this land
some hearts too full of sand
with pearls glimmering grand
touch my bosom
with a blossom
of innocented truth
smile me with thy humour
kiss me with thy splendour
the armour of yours
remove and brace me with fibres
figure of mine at ease dines
with pining mates de-wined
brush me not

my breasts shall bleed
slap not my cheeks
yours will sharply creek
I am but starving blind
give me some heart in kind.

MY SKIN STRETCHED OUT TO MEET YOU

I extended my arms
pulling out my skin
like a lump of cloth
love soaked, ovumed
when night was on
my skin refused
to stretch longer
all the way to you
I wrung them dry
and folded into a napkin

When we awoke
I stretched myself out
like a sun carpet
my skin lunged forward
to meet you
my lips hugged your mouth
but missed your smiles
when I circled my fingers
around your bosom's width
you were not there.

My skin is waiting still
like a virgin egg

"The Lord God made garments of skin for Adam and his wife, and
clothed them." (Genesis 3.21)

PART – V

THE FORBIDDEN FRUITS

TASTE OF EXOTIC & UNKNOWN

BE A CO-TRAVELER

Caught between the devil and the deep sea I am dying. Either I suffer from bereavement or drowned and soaked I get wet forever eternally drowned. What to do, I am too much in love that I am burning with love. O Lord, guide me to the other shore…

A poet is the one who keeps plenty of secrets and sometimes spontaneously he begins to sing in his soul and then writes them down. When he forgets himself and writes it becomes a poem which touches and sometimes converts the reader.

Do not first buy, but just be a co-traveler, in the roads of life, in the road to heaven, have a passer-by who shall forever be a companion who needs no explanation for smiling or crying. Have a hand, that knows when to support, have a heart that knows when to throb, have a lip that knows when to kiss or not to. Have a hug that knows when to or not to. Do not buy, but be a fellow good Samaritan. After all life is only a ladder to reach God's paradise.....

AND THE RED WINE

He placed
deep red ruby gems
upon my lips

Tantalizing is my tongue,
senses so seductive

The candle, lights my face
with flares of gold

And the red wine
is so thirsty.

"Forbidden to you are your mothers, your daughters, sisters, father's sisters, mother's sisters, brother's daughters, sister's daughters, foster mother who gave you suck, foster milk suckling sisters, your wives' mothers, your step daughters under your guardianship, born of your wives to whom you have gone in, wives of your sons who spring from your own loins, and two sisters in wedlock at the same time, except for what has already passed; verily, Allah is Oft-Forgiving, Most Merciful. (سورة النساء, An-Nisaa 4.23)

MY BODY ICE CREAM

Melting
at sight
of delight
juicy
watering
at touch of lips
who made you
sweet maid,
laying slyly
yonder in the
cool bar bins

Flavours
smell all over
your body
soft and supple
as I lick you
up and down
hugging me
with mounting taste
oh my dear
too sweet I swear!

Heart of Yours
disheartens me
as I know
you are half way through
in a frenzied urge
I kiss you down
to touch the crap
of wooden cups

all ended
before I could
even think of it
just a lightning streak
you went through my beak
like a silver fish
before I decided
you faded.

"He should take the semen with his ring finger and thumb and rub it between his breasts or eyebrows, repeating the mantra: "Let the semen return to me, let Vigour come to me again, let glow and good fortune come to me again. May the deities who dwell in the sacrificial fire put the semen back in its proper place." (Brihadaranyak Upanishad 6.4.5)

WILL YOU TASTE MY LOVE

When the roses wait
for kiss of the dew
when first rays of sun
touch the tiny beaks
of singing love birds
when in my soft smiling lips
and in my shining eyes
you see thousand little stars
hiding in my soul

secretly

would you taste my ardent love
flowing from my moist mouth
and give me a soft kiss
on my aching lips
and kindle my tongue with desire
whose memory will lead me
from this glorious dawn
through to the dusk?

"Verily, those who want illegal **sex**ual intercourse to be propagated among those who believe, they will have a painful torment in this world and in the Hereafter. And Allah knows and you know not." (سورة النور, An-Noor 24.19)

TASTE OF OUR FIRST KISS

I still remember the evening
we walked down to the river
near the wild forest flowers
bordering our little village

As we sat under a flower tree
on this evening of beatitude
the sun became orange gold
and took a crimson hue of pink
before going down suddenly
below the dark edges of distant hills

Here we kissed for the first time

You are not here now
but still I feel the taste
of the lukewarm saltiness
of your flickering tongue
on my parched lips

This salt is more than real
I feel your lips on my lips
your chest on my breasts
your kiss spreading down
my whole being on fire

"Marry those among you who are single - a man who has no wife and
woman who has no husband - and also marry the pious ones among your
slaves and maid-servants. If they be poor, Allah will enrich them out of His
Bounty. And Allah is All-Sufficient for His creatures' needs, All-Knowing."
(سورة النور, An-Noor 24.32)

SALT ON MY LIPS

It is more than the real
memory of our last kiss
etched in salt on my lips
you are here in ethereal
mystified loving presence

you appear no more
at my soul's call
I invoke your memory
and your kiss appears
wearing your smile
dripping old love
all salt and brine

a single quick lick
and my lips are on fire
this brine is enough
to kindle my flame
heat envelopes me
like sizzling salt pans
simmering under sun

I feel ecstatic with desire
at this hour of noon.

"Thereafter we made the offspring of Adam as a Nutfah mixed drops of the male and female **sex**ual discharge, and lodged it in a safe lodging in womb of the woman." (سورة المؤمنون, Al-Muminoon 23.13)

I PINE FOR YOUR NECTAR

My lips thirst for the nectar
oozing from your orifice
my flesh pines for you
Don't you see
How I pine, pine?

Allow me to graze my lips
on the nectar of your orifice
quenching the fire of thirst
in the honeycombs of desire
let me find my love's solace

Cast me not away, beloved
From the nectar of your youth
Give me just a little place
In the great expanse
Of your beautiful heart

My lips shall glorify you
they will sing of you
with exultant leaps
of emotions unbound
my mouth shall praise
the nectar of your lips.

"You say, 'Food was made for stomach, and stomach for food.' This is true, though someday God will do away with both of them. But you can't say that our bodies were made for sexual immorality. They were made for the Lord, and the Lord cares about our bodies." **(Corinthians 6:13)**

MAY I TASTE YOUR SUN LIPS

May I embrace you first
A tight and intense embrace
Before we enter into lip lock
Of divine love?

You dance with soft steps
And slowly take me to sudden gusts
Of desire turning to warm love
And I enjoy it like the lotus
At the first rays of the sun

Then in a moment of deep love
You sink into my waiting mouth
Like a weasel into the waterhole
Your lips are warm and moist
And my eyes are filled with joy

I feel your whispers in my ears
My hairs love your fingers now
Weaving melodies of desire
As your lips begin to dance
On the skin of my parched tongue

I forget all that is mundane
And fly to the high heavens
To tell my Guardian Angel
'I have found my true love'.

"For while we were in the flesh, the sinful passions, which were aroused
by the Law, were at work in the members of our body to bear fruit for."
(Romans 7.5)

KISS ON OCEAN BED

Ocean beds are dangerous
sharks and seals
together stick
for a game of lick
deep down under
yet, strongly it haunts you
the call of sea
the blue waves
their magic curves
massaging kiss
dark modest wish
and salty aftermath
of brush of lips
little by little
haunted by the witch
you step in
and step into…

a mindless cavern
of limitless darkness
punctuated in stripes
by spots of desire.

"If our minds are ruled by our desires, we will die. But if our minds are ruled by the Spirit, we will have life and peace." **(Romans 8:6)**

KISS ME WITH LIPS OF YOUR HEART

Kiss me with your heart
lips are little devils,
they make us slaves
instead of queens,
they promise us
bonded intoxication
Kiss me with your heart
touch my emotions deep
softily, softily, softily
look into my hurt eyes
the bleeding ones that ache
from deep within,
from childhood
balm them,
oh balm them
tie my wounds
unknown to me
unseen by me
but found by you
with the light in your looks
that lighten up with love's warmth
kiss me with your heart
with your love bands clean
with hygiene lips of heart
touch the pains
inside my brains
and heal the scars
sown by hands
unknown to you,
unseen by you
yet, for the sake of my love

for the sake of your love
kiss me with your heart
orange lips of your heart
give me the strength to live
Give me the strength to love.

"Now flee from youthful lusts and pursue righteousness, faith, love and peace, with those who call on the Lord from a pure heart." (Tomothy 2.22)

FLAVOUR OF DESIRE

soft and supple
your cream body
curved around me
flavoured all over

as I licked you
up and down
hugging you
with mounting desire
oh my dear
too sweet I swear!

"Beloved, I urge you as aliens and strangers to abstain from fleshly lusts
which wage war against the soul." (Peter 2.11)

PART – VI

THE PERFUME GARDEN
EARTHLY SMELL OF LOVE

TWO HALVES OF GOD

Two is joy. In creation everything is created in only two. Even the sprouting bud comes in twos. Sun and moon, day and night, two ears, two nostrils, two eyes, two cheers, two legs, two hands, two lungs, two hearts make one love. Two breasts for a single child. Two ovaries for a single uterus, two cheeks for a single face. And Two was God split into when he wanted to make Love

For ages I have been kept hungry and imprisoned in a cave. Now you are filling the parched deserted heart with heavenly ambrosia. Oh god, when divine energies flood in, what could mortal souls say. Now you are feeding this famished soul, whose intestine's capacity is just a hole of blue sky and a pinch of golden sun light. You are filling my whole with ocean of love when my heart's capacity is that of a newborn baby to suckle just a drop of its flavour.

I am every day morning brushing their teeth, oiling their hair, combing, powdering, milking them, feeding them, clothing them, caressing and fondling them, laugh with them, show them sky, birds, mongoose, owls, bats and all that my eyes could see, sing songs to them, kiss them with my loving heart. What not I do for them. Now when I open my heart and show to you, you say oh, it is only a shoe flower..."

SECRET FRAGRANCE OF HUGS

The damp roots of earth
hug and kiss secretly
in their dark chambers
emitting a secret fragrance
unknown to lovers on earth

Desire for secret romance
wells up in their hearts
and sand around the roots
begins to hug earnestly
along their hidden widths
and secret lengths
of unspoken desire

They are busy now
hugging and kissing
stem to stem, root to root
in a royal romance

The lovers inhaled it
deep under ground
with the smell of earth,
were tickled by its waft
and furtively smiled.

"In the pleasure room, decorated with flowers, and fragrant with perfumes, a man should receive his woman, who should come bathed and dressed, and invite her to take refreshments and drinks. He should seat her on his left, and holding her hair, he should gently embrace her with his right arm…" (Kama Sutra)

EARTH'S SWEET SMELL OF LUST

How sweet is the smell
of Earth - it's heart and shell
the clothing soil
in every turmoil
when it rains
sends out a smell
of life and lust
awfully scented
the virgin blended
could Earth have Sex
with Heavens above
how springs flowers
and sprouts out shrubs
when breasts of clouds
bursts open by cooled airs
Earth smells
not of RDX grenades
and nuclear fumes
but of life's sweetest seeds

"Therefore consider the members of your earthly body as dead to immorality, impurity, passion, evil desire, and greed, which amounts to idolatry." (Colossians 3.5)

ODOR OF YOUR MANLY SWEAT

My love
when you hugged me
with the hairy mansion of yours
the odour of manly sweat
as it outpoured
my life you did make complete
i found the meaning
and mission of life
all aches stopped sudden
and the arches craved
and curved starved
the cot was no more in the skies
down to earth did I come
i found every empty words come true
and thus we had a babe of two
lovely little sweetest kid
who i kiss remembering you
recalling that night
I still fondle his full round face
and caress his soft pink cheeks
for you are only now a memory
the days of passion are over
my limbs are aching
and hands are shaking
my naked body is shivering
i am but waiting
waiting for the call of death
my days are numbered
yet, how lusty were those lovely days
when you tell me, I too intake
the beautiful nights and blinded days

into one wonderful dream
I too swim for creams
yet my dear,
life is too short
and your briefs only just for a brief
sadly bying you, my lust is in dust
i am bying forever....

"A man alone is nothing — he is incomplete. The perfect man is one who is completely united in harmony with his wife and children. These three are ONE. (Manu Smriti 9.45)

SECRET CHAMBER OF MUSIC AND SCENT

Night is silent
though earth is awake
Men are sleeping
birds are nested
the air speaks in tender tones
touch the harp in the heart
it tells of stories of the past
the moonlit paths
starry delights
the merry lives
and the dancing prides
now the midnight bells
sounds lovely calls
how sweet the air
responds to the charm
of jingling bells
fairies and angels
faintly appear
you walk along beaches
the roars sink you
with mysterious creatures
some in the air, some in water
some lands, some distants
Nights is Spiritual
full of drunken melodies
and emptying stories
sleepless torments
too suck life energies
now, you can stretch your limbs
on the deserted strings
to watch the nobody lands

and fill your lungs
with living winds
full of music and scents
from faraway trends
births and rebirths
have traced and retraced
paths of life
every night is beautiful
the secret chambers all full

"Ganikaputra says that, as a rule a woman falls in love with every handsome man she sees, and so does every man at the sight of beautiful woman. But frequently the man and woman do not take any further steps due to various considerations. A woman loves without regard to right or wrong. She does not try to gain over a man just for attainment of any particular purpose. Moreover, when a man first approaches her she naturally shrinks from him, eventhough she may be willing to unite herself with him." (Kama Sutra)

I SMELT THE STARLIT NIGHTS

On starlight nights
all alone I sat
like a bride in waiting
on a small rock
smelling of wet earth
near the little rivulet
that was flowing peacefully
near the fields of flower

Looking into the sky
I saw little white stars
twinkling like loose petals
on my warm nuptial bed
waiting for me
talking to my body
in whispers of love

When I looked around
I saw only dark fields
stretching endlessly
to horizon and beyond
solitude engulfed me
in its vast blackness

The earth alone gave warmth
To my cold naked feet
with its assuring fragrance
of moist secret love
mixed with warm
wet desire

How I wish to be a bride
in the arms of my beloved
on the firmament of desire
how I wish to come
on his musk's prompting
how I wish to spring
from my secret crannies
the sweet smell of wet earth.

A TALE OF SMELL

The dawn smiles
deep inside me
in the morning
when I wake up
after the dark night
as if they were waiting for me
the buds tell
a tale of smell
within their
yet to open infant fingers

the morning birds
start singing
when they see me peep
from my window sill
charged with life
they start colouring
with watery shades

its rainy season;
no dews,
but the tiny leaf blades
have stolen pearls
gems of drops
from the icy rains
at night

"If she meets him once, and again comes to meet him better dressed than before, or comes to him in some lonely place, he should be certain that she is capable of being enjoyed by him." (Kama Sutra)

MUSK OF EDEN

My desires anchored
at the Garden of Eden
halt for the night
row no further
let me now take rest
in the aroma of love
wafting from its gates

before I enter
I wish to replenish
my old desires
with fresh love
I do not wish now
to go inside
with my old longings
let the musk brew
in secret overnight
into a fervent concoction

Let the night pass
in secret sweetness
by dawn I shall enter
my garden of love
to kill my desire
with old musk.

"If she happens to go to sleep in his vicinity, he should put his left arm
around her, and see when she awakes whether she repulses him in reality,
or only repulses him in a way as if she was desirous of the same thing
being done to her again." (Kama Sutra)

LOVE ODOR IN DARKNESS

Fumbling around
I found my moorings
in the dark crevices
of my own desire

It is noon and dark
moist warm weeds
slither in profusion
sticking to the walls
of my secret garden
with a gluey stickiness
making them slippery
with the mad odor of
sunburnt armpits

deep your fingers
with a wavy motion
through the curtains
of my vault of darkness

feel my darkness
feel me down there
with your longing
smell my desires
ripe with warm odor
from the dark corners
of your moist fingernails

"May Lord Vishnu make your womb ready; may the celestial craftsman design the shape of the embryo. May the Lord of Beings activate the sperm and may the Creator grant conception." (Atharva 5.25.5)

SMELL MY RIVER OF DESIRE

Like a river in flood
my desires flow
knowing no bounds
I overflow
at my bends
with my own perfume load

come
flow with me
like a tributary
mingle in me
add to my perfumes
your fresh fragrance of love

Halt in my sand banks
look, here my flow is soft
caress my softer sides
with your love pedals
whip up the currents
into a powerful flow

Smell me
around my corners
the juniper in my breasts
honey in my lips
musk in the navel
smell of wild berries
in my arms' reaches

before I join you
at the furthest bend

PERFUME GARDEN

She was crying
alone by herself
haunched all over
her earthen dreams

Her perfume bottles
were spilt all over
the velvet garden
of monsoon green

un stoppered
her perfume was leaking
in wafer thin wafts
of mild desire

I picked up a scent
on a silent cue
from her moist eyes
It led me to a flower
blooming in a crevice
smelling of secret passion

Passion flower it was
she whispered to me
when later at night
gathering her scents
she came to me
behind the garden
and we embraced.

THE LAST FRAGRANCE

It is fainter
but sweeter
memories of your
last fragrance

I am digging into my skin
to find the furthest reach
of your sweet smell of love

come, meet me
my love
meet me in my nights
when I am longing
for you the most

When I meet you
I shall rekindle in me
the memories of your
last fragrance

"He created man from Nutfah (mixed drops of male and female **sex**ual discharge), and now see, this same man has becomes an open opponent." (سورة النحل, An-Nahl 16.4)

BOOK TWO

THE FOUR SEASONS

SEX AND SIN

KISS OF LIFE

TEMPLE OF LOVE

I AM PREGNANT

Now when evening came David arose from his bed and walked around on the roof of the king's house. And from the roof he saw a woman bathing. The woman was very beautiful in appearance. So David sent and inquired about the woman. And one said, "Is this not Bathsheba, the daughter of Eliam, the wife of Uriah the Hittite?"

David sent messengers and took her, and when she came to him, he lay with her; and when she had purified herself from her uncleanness, she returned to her house.

The woman conceived; and she sent and told David, and said, "I am pregnant." (Samuel 11.2-5)

PART – VII

THE FOUR SEASONS

LOVE IN RAIN AND SUNSHINE

NIGHT OF THE CROSS BEARER

You are the god I was searching for. What more could I say. If a human heart could be divine, if god is born as human and if you could sense his heart, then it is yours. I had never in the horizon of my dreams horizon ever dreamed that a man could be as divine as you. And to be truthful, the man behind the curtain of god, I kneel before him too.

Never, never shall I betray you. Though a lamb you are a lamp. You are my dearest Jesus. You are the lone light at the top of my temple. And I shall never never even show you any cross at all. You see, I am the biggest cross in the world. Then you know, this cross if you wear, if you endure, then no cross will be more difficult for you to bear.

The cross will be thrown out soon. And it will have to walk to the cross bearer in the middle of night. Hope the cross bearer will come riding a white peacock to me....

You are my be-all and end-all.

MONSOON LOVE

Every drop is divinely formed
needling down the grey sky
are some scaled drops lining straight
some are gushing forth like school children
no time to waste, once expelled out of cloudy dens
some float upon the laps of gusty winds
and kiss upon the greedy leaves
rain drops fall with lovely emotions
the rarest are the ones that fashions
just after the hottest Summer season
smell of earth, smell of earth
in childhood days we used to hearth
those were days when rains were new
and nascent earth smelt fresh anew
every change in nature stirred new passion
to paint, to dance, to sing wild with action
tip, tip, upon the leafy hearts
taps the drops melting her pots

Monsoon season is god's own passion
as rain descends, lust ascends
every flame is ignited
every mate seeks to be united
nameless urges surges drugged
every bird chirps with fresh charm
every bed is warm and a wonder alarm
rain sings before it falls
upon the hilly trends where water travels slow
its a marvel to hear the sound of rain
like a whisper from heavenly terrains
hissing serpents from yonder sky

they set loose your every desire delayed
When rain drops fall, I want to skate
from top to bottom through their skirts
sometimes I wonder if water goes up or down
or is it a magnetic needle drawing every cool form
directly into its own core endlessly adorned.

"Soma became desirous of a wife. Both Ashvins became harbingers.
When Surya became desirous of groom, Savita mentally offered her to
him." (Rg Veda 10.85.9)

RAIN WET NIGHTS

Like a virgin bride
after a lovely night
earth awoke
to rainy delights.

How beautiful
are the touches of life!
rain wet nights
the music all night
it drums into your soul
the vibrant music
of the wild breeze
the hissing leaves
the howling wind
the passion,
the intoxicant urge
it blows out the candle of imagination
the titanic battles of nature
they vanquish your dreamy fairy tales
your wildest imaginations cant sketch
or paint or fabricate
the beauty personified by nature's lust

Rain washed
a lovely mother she is our earth
born are millions of babies
her womb every fertile
yet she is charming and seductive
Rains are more than what eyes view
some demonic angelic heart
hugs to every rainy drop

watching rain in its fullest pour
makes you feel life-past and future explored
I melt into nothing washed by rain
in and out I just drift along with the downpours
emotions flood out, images dance, childhood jumps out
youth makes impish appearances
my greying old age wiped by torrents of triggered fences.

"When the child is born, he prepares the fire, places the child on his lap, and having poured thick milk mixed with ghee into a metal jug, he sacrifices it bit by bit, saying: "May I, as I increase my house, nourish a thousand! May fortune never fail in his race, with offspring and cattle."

"I offer to thee in my mind the vital breaths which are in me. Whatever in my work I have done too much, or whatever I have here done too little, may Agni make this right and proper for us, Svaha!" (Brihad 6.4.24)

MELTING IN LOVE RAINS

Needling
probing
pricking
piercing
pi nching
pilfering
peeping
pinning
pict urising
pinking, inking
bleeding
bubbling
bullying
bul ldozing
buffooning
buttering
basking, budding
oh no, rains are my favourites
Monsoon comes and I go
I just surrender at the feet of Monsoon sky

What do rains do?
I don't know,
but sure, they drill me in and out
they kill me and enliven me
they ransack my emotions and passions
raid my past, present and future dreams
take me out part by part
and hang them up in zoomed lot
every inch of my being is being tossed up
and looked by a magnifying glass cup

oh rains, rain clouds, thunder and storm
lightning and hurricanes
they just wipe me out
whip up every single urge within
I want to hug the entire world
the lovely squirrels, the twittering birds,
the untouchable skies, the undiggable earth
the ponds, the oceans, the rivers and brooks
and mountain peaks and hills and horizon beds
Rains they wet me in and out, make me hot and cold
I am freezing and fuelling all at the same time
wow, just melting and solidifying in one single flame
all air speaking in the summitting volumes
liquidifying my being to hear, listen
and reply and respond with inner vibrations
I react without any stop, involuntarily shaking
my whole body ignited, enflamed, I wild and crazy
oh, the rains are penetrating into my very privacy.

"The earth is the essence of all these things, water is the essence of the
earth plants of water, flowers of plants, fruits of flowers, man of fruits, seed
of man." (Brihadaranyak Upanishad 6.4.1)

MONSOON RIPPLES IN POND OF LIFE

Painted by monsoon rain
waters are turquoise green;
who will paint the pond's face
but monsoon rain with mossy surface
Green and clear beauty of pond is seductive
mirroring all vibrations around
reflecting the blue sky
green leaves and full moon amply
I love of all the things she shows
her lovely ripples coupling and singling.

Ripple, the word is a beauty
triggered by hands unknown
hearts unthought of
messages unasked for
moods and stimuli appear, disappear
what a beauty, the ripple in the pond.
a drop from above the coconut leaves
splash of king fisher that plunges to fashion
and licks of air that dries it commotion
the swimming tortoises
the swarm of fishes
every little being triggers ripples
in my heart's sanctuary
like a woman's heart
in love ripples of delight.

"If a man wishes that a reddish son with tawny eyes should be born to him,
and that he should know two Vedas, and live to his full age, then, after
having prepared boiled rice with coagulated milk and butter, they should
both eat, being fit to have offspring." (Brihad 6.4.15)

SUN IN LAP OF SUMMER MOON

When my sun was lost in night's lap
I wept and wept till my heart broke;
And slept in my tears all wet and woke
as midnight rose something touched stroked
and the silvery hands hugged my fours
your rude sun am I
touched by your love
I am transformed into a moon
full of melting eloquence
and mellifluous dreams
but night alone shall I come
darkness alone could see me spun
those magic loves in hearts of fun
to you alone I am the dreamy dove
to the world around she said
I am the sun all bright
blazing in the summer
of moon's delight.

"Now the deeds of the flesh are evident, which are: immorality, impurity, sensuality, idolatry, sorcery, enmities, strife, jealousy, outbursts of anger, disputes, dissensions, factions, envying, drunkenness, carousing, and things like these, of which I forewarn you, just as I have forewarned you, that those who practice such things will not inherit the kingdom of God." (Galatians 5.19-21)

VIRGIN SMELL OF SUMMER SKIES

painted red
in the memory wall
is the Juicy call
of yester lives

young alive
the air was fresh
the sky was blue
the moon was full
the song was sweet

very touch was an imprint
very look was an album
very sight was a film
very taste was Superb!

when God was a Virgin
smelling innocence
and toyed with eternal sense
then smiles were sprouting
like stars in the summer skies

limbs were dancing
likes were twitching
hearts were squealing
hopes were skating

the glimmer in the eyes
the glitter in the looks
the twitter in the tone
and the butter in those fakes

buds are full of hopes
unripened seeds are
future's fruits
uncorked bottle
treasures the tastiest Eve

Dreams are made of pasts
when Age is greying fast
Tomorrows are born of yesterdays
yet, yesterdays roots of Tomorrows
water them, feed them, the dried trunk of fate....

"When a man and a woman are very much in love with each other, and, without thinking of pain or hurt, embrace each other as though they were entering each other's body, either while the woman is sitting on the man's lap or in front of him, or both on a bed, then it is called an embrace like a 'mixture of milk and water'. (Kama Sutra)

RAIN BRIDE OF DESIRE

drops of moisture
filling the air
cleansing the view
with washing crew

when it rains
cooling earth grains
songs of heart multiplies
hearths of fire intensifies

the nights are deep and swollen
with whispers of soft leaves fallen
days are disappearing fast
underneath the umbrellas of raining past

when rains arrive
ruined dreams alive
haunted mind is set astride
hunted scars pain the bride...

"If a man see himself in the water, he should recite the mantra : "May there be in me splendour, strength, glory, wealth, virtue." She is the best of women whose garments are pure. Therefore let him approach a woman whose garments are pure, and whose fame is pure, and address her." (Brihadaranyak Upanishad 6.4.6)

FERTILITY DREAMS IN RAIN

I love to watch the sight of rain
sketching long lines in air
needles of water, distinct and clear
definite and sure what to do
no matter whoever hate it touch
and hurries up before it reaches dressed.

Rain is ringing in fertility in lives
birds love and date and court with monsoons
dipping in waters of ponds they delight
watching their jumps makes me punch.

How happy are those wanderers on sky
we with metallic wings sigh
but they with no nest of fixed rest
they float across the oceanic depths
watch how beautifully they glide along
their feathers fanning wide apart.

Rain brings in hungers
to eat, to sleep, to mate, to recreate
fresh ideas tumble down, free life erupts
drenched hearts are fertility's field
touch not those drops
without touching me deep.

Editor's Note :- Hemangi Sharma wrote it on July 17, 2015 – just a week before she met me for the first time in person. She said those were her happiest days.

RAINS HAVE A PAGE IN MY LIFE

I am lazy;
I am cozy;
leaning against my easy chair
with my legs held upon a stool rare
my being looped
to look at the sky
with clouds of urging cries
how they vanish?
how they appear?
breezed in
and squeezed out
what lovely emotions
the speechless marvels carry through
Rains!
oh! Many a legends
many a creative hearths
many a births and
many a deaths
many a chilling partings
walking alone in the rainy nights
Rains have a page in every man's life
the nameless moods
that assemble the brains
now i want to eat
next i want to heat
my numb legs
and nestling thighs
then i want to coil inside
with my kiddies under a blanky
watching movies
under the nets

SUMMER RAINS

I can't refuse
It is Summer Rain
when the Earth
shuns the heat
and the blazing heat
kills her heart
then comes the refuge
the cooling drops
from the breasts of love
they taste the aroma of life
refill with energy to live
the mating urge is born
in the huts and mansions huge
the hormones swell
and honey bees dwell
upon the blooms
to suckle the nectar
oozing from the pool
to be possessed
of the frenzied natural urge
and be under the seize of eternal lust
Raining, Raining, Raining
Oh my heart, my head
My endless pining.

"If a man wishes that a dark son should be born to him with red eyes, and
that he should know three Vedas, and live to his full age, then, after having
prepared boiled rice with water and butter, they should both eat, being fit
to have offspring." (Brihad 6.4.16)

RAIN SHADOWS ON SOFT BREASTS

whistling and whispering
inside my thick dark covers
longing to play card games
with clouds circling around
let me smile now in peace
as memories ease

the air is sticky
as if each atom licks
some soft breast
yielding milky chest
some yearning of distant teens
some 'if onlys' hovering and haunting

gloomy shadows
now trail behind
lurking behind curtains' shade
listening to some pessimistic maid
sobbing over sinking tides
every man and woman rides
in reins of monsoon bride
some in glee, some unfree
some drunken, some sunken
some stubbornly refusing
to yield to the storming rings.

"If a man wishes that a learned son should be born to him, famous, a public man, a popular speaker, that he should know all the Vedas, and that he should live to his full age, then, after having prepared boiled rice with meat and butter, they should both eat, being fit to have offspring. The meat should be of a young ox or of an old bull." (Brihad 6.4.18)

SUNSHINE ON MY MONSOON LOVE

After years of penance
rains came
pouring heavily
lashing right and left
leaving nothing untouched
just jumping from heavenly orifices
water drops of different types
round, big, lined, diffusive,
straight, soft, husky, rayed, blown out
like a whisper
slap, pat, galloping horse
tigering for prey
in many forms did rain came
dancing, singing, laughing, wetting our souls
we can't resist the urge to kiss
the mounting passions, mad and crazy
rains penetrated into the being inside
we were carried away to worlds unseen
some angelic delight, some demonic hiss
hugging me with her cooling gaze
rain was beautiful, terrific, tearing apart
and inventing new I-s,
I was like a ballet dancer
in a vortex of uncontrolled passion
in an avalanche of destiny
fierce and fondly stroking
I was turned inside out
all that was inhibition's treasure
auctioned free to public eye

but that was not my urge to write
it is today's sunshine that made me pen
like a lazy queen
waking up from her legendary slumber
monsoon gave chance for earth to speak
she woke up nature with her natural beauties
every leaf glistening with energetic lustre
every being of green with lusty ember
the whole nature purified by rains shone
sun light licking every audible groan
the song of wind was sweet
whipping up every unknown tweet.

I don't know what to do with my ugly physique
everything is ethereal and angelic
priceless and precious hours dawned again
when sun intervenes monsoon session
the heart overwhelmed with impatient urges
but poor mind knows not what to do
the whole being quivers to nature's music
I am defeated, captured, captivated,
I surrender, my will melting, i am sinking
I want to die at this moment of life
when everything is so sweet and pure
when nature's virgin innocence
seals my conscious sure.

"O Surya, Brahmins know about your two seasonal cycles. But one of
these cycles which is secret, is known only to the seer." (Rg Veda
10.85.16)

SUMMER CALLS

After ages
rains come out
like an infant
born after years of marriage
so softly the summer crept in
nobody noticed that winter has glided by
heat consumed energies
and nature came with the cure
how beautiful are the dark clouds
when they come for the first time
the sky pregnant with cooling pillows
the air full of hopes and expectations.
birds are chirping with a new music
my heart is thumping with a new lyric
the alterations in the Cuckoos call
the variations in the sparrows squeal
oh how beautifully nature speaks to nature
The rain air is hugging my interiors
and I am drenched within before without.

"If a man wishes that a learned daughter should be born to him, and that she should live to her full age, then, after having prepared boiled rice with sesamum and butter, they should both eat, being fit to have offspring." (Brihad 6.4.17)

WET DREAMS IN MY LOVE FOREST

Wet am I
earth too;
somewhere deep beneath
heart is melting to molten tears
all fears gone
insecurities wiped of
speaks the voice of calm
with lovely gentle charm.
the tap of rain
upon the green breasts
gems of white
they glisten and ball around
the untied bonds of leaves

When it rains
thoughts rain
a new world dawns
birds mate with fervent urge
new lusts are born with faithless haste
earth is shaken with umpteen passions
the urge to sprout competes
in every microcosmic being
man to woman, worm to worm
pig to she pig, frog to frog lady
earth is ringing with bells of alarms
very very deep within the genes
urge to produce kills the lethargies
igniting hot feelings is the cold rain

How to express how rain touches?
its a long long story-a legendary tale

a mystery, the arrival of monsoon
and the washing off of Summer's heart
the consuming sun, the liquidating temperatures
now, the rain with consummating energy
all cool cool arrives with drowning emotions
and sinking disturbances
remember the little paper boat
the ice stones pelting once in a year
the first rainbow in your childhood days
the first sapling, the first kingfisher you saw
the first love of your school days
the first Mills and Boon you read
Anyway, topping it all rain is a exhaustive lady
she has her never ending charms and deceptive harms
transparent she is a beauty in herself
her multiple dimensions awesome
the breeze her knight in arm
he persuades her to kindle earth
with a world of mushrooming versions
of procreative emulsions
her charms blow off your mind and heart
I am still a slave of the monsoon start
like a tiny Lilliputian I watch and watch
and admire and admire
I grow tinier and tinier
she like a giant avatar dances wildly
and I reduced to insanity
pygmified blink with my zero stability.

"Even if this much semen—of one asleep or of one awake—is spilled, he
should touch it and repeat the mantra: "Whatever semen of mine has spilt
on earth, whatever has flowed to plants, whatever to water, I reclaim it."
(Brihad 6.4.5)

MOONLIT DELIGHTS

When rainy clouds black and bleak
skirted my sky with venomous streak
and downpours plagued my lovely earth
with outflowing sewages full of stench
I was depressed and moaned in and out
my friends I lost touch with
and smiles were rare to be seen
as everyone was helpless and crazy
just to reach home was infinitely lazy
the day was full of freezing coldness
all hot life sickened with muddy mundanities
life became soaked with definite sadness
that was coated with melancholy and madness.

Soon the day fell into nights lap
and bloomed the lily of the silver isles
moon came out in splendour dressed in the bright
her charms reborn, with refreshing fervour
the moon light gave me exquisite delight
I just revived my dying spirits
for she came with a beautiful light
that descended from heavenly sights
like the kiss of a baby, soft and sublime
the moon lit night harped upon earths face
with a tender lace of faith and optimistic rays.

"The curved mark with the nails, which a lover impresses on the neck and breasts of a woman, is called the 'half moon'. When the half moons are impressed opposite to each other, it is called a 'circle'. Such marks with nails are generally made on the navel, the small cavities about the buttocks, and on the thigh." (Kama Sutra)

LUNAR LIASIONS

Moon smiles on waveletful ocean
In myriad nisi but surfeit oscillation
Fiancée's face in veritable vibration
Heart in rhapsodic constellations.
Aquatic n' Lunar liaison
Metaphorically in coalition
Solacing in blissful pavilion
Why in realm of obfuscation
Souse in fête fiancée unison.

My body arches with the tension
Your touch brought in its wake
My limbs too feel a gentle shake
Taught breasts shine like full moons
In love's secret sweet anticipation

Come love come
Spring has given way to Summer
Spring has given way to Summer

Note :- This poem signalled Hemangi Sharma's break with her past and arrival of new love in her life.

"O you who believe! When you marry believing women, and then divorce them before you have **sex**ual intercourse with them, you need not count Iddah period for them. So give them a present, and set them free in a handsome manner." (سورة الأحزاب, Al-Ahzaab 33.49)

PASSION AFTER THE RAINS

Watch Rain
and you feel it in your brains
close your eyes
you can feel the cool leaves
before it rains in hills
their whiskers brush with airs
mustache tickles the country bowers
swirling dust and fallen leaves
they hunt your heart like howling elfs
roaming wind rocks your mind
round and round the message is sent
and every tree passes the word
and Apps is switched on
every leaf big and small, tiny and large
expectant of augmenting rain
claps their branches
and giggles the buds and sprouting boughs
clouds peer and clap their thunders
heavens lighten their passionate wonders
Rain is coming and life rich with powers.
sweet mud, fragrant veiled like a virgin bride
waiting the drops to penetrate into her bed
the first rain drops finishes the famishing maid
Like the climax of a story and climbing music reaching its height
The pinnacles of nature's beauty stretching to mysterious wilds
Here Comes Rain bouncing in ecstasy and hankers of lusty ride.

After Rain
watch the cleansed clouds
the azure sky, pure and dried
the calm earth, with no signs of fights

leaves modestly jeweled with liquid life
roots eagerly sucking the water sweet
birds flirting and dating upon the trees
all around the aroma of passion quenched
wind is nowhere, storm is silent,
air has no quivers, moist is her breast
washed with neatness like new born uniforms
all greens are impeccably white
ponds are precious clear
It peeps out of the light streaming from hidden sun bear
life's symphony now halting for low decibels unheard
After the rains everything is new born
all virgin greens pregnant with passion's babies tuned.

"If a man wishes that a white son should be born to him, and that he should
know one Veda, and live to his full age, then, after having prepared boiled
rice with milk and butter, they should both eat, being fit to have offspring."
(Brihad 6.4.14)

BLUSHING UNDER SUN KISSES

The golden blushes
brushes the green leaves washed
by all night pour sweet and strong
the dawn awoke too early
every green sparkling in delight
the earlier birds hummed her spirit
with energetic music filling life and space
When the sun peeps in
after the freezing night
cold and damp when rain drizzles you to death
even a ray of miserly smile feasts
the whole pond of green mirrors beauty
the ray of light that follows adversity
its like the faith of a follower
the hope of a drowning heart
what a sight it is to watch
after the horrible mundane drab life
when the sun hugs you tight
showering kisses left and right

Nature is God's own teacher
why beat students for not learning stupid lessons
wisdom flows from nature's cyclic sensitivity
watch the vibrant leaves flutter deep within
butterflies dating with every golden hue
courting birds chirping out the purest love
for every rain, there is a Sun
that rains out faith in life
and fills out cheer and joy.

MUSIC RIPPLES ON MY BODY POND

On my curves the music jingles like bangles
watch the ripples come again and again
I love the concentric circles
the way they spread to distant corners
how emotions are sent through e-mails
and how thoughts are carried by telepathic trails
the physics and chemistry are all nature's bounty
the longitudinal wavelets,
giggles of kids happy and wild
born of touch of airy fairies blind
they loose their path and waters guide.

Pond to me is a panorama of life
not for the birds and lives that throng its shore
not for the watery lives within it stores
but for the magnanimity it resounds
capturing every life and beauty around
how it appears like a repertoire of classics
of biodiversity that surrounds
I feel there is life in those waters
waters that speak out in tongues of ripples
some day, some time, may be if I ask some question silly
she may ripple the reply out to me to tell it
to children who sleep in concrete indoors
and make them wake up to her secret stores.

"Auddalika says – Females do not emit as males do. Males simply remove their desires, while the females, from their consciousness of desire, feel a certain kind of pleasure which gives them satisfaction. But it is impossible for them to tell you what kind of pleasure they feel." (Kama Sutra)

MY GARDEN OF SPRINGS

Yester night
when moon was a delight
and soft romance in flight
on my dream bed did alight
the gardener was busy
his hopes were all rosy
and seeds were very pushy
the soil was checked out
no weeds was made out
solid paths charted out
landscape was road rollered
the pit and peaks scaled
mounds were mastered to electric shrieks
endless earthquakes consumed the make
long after the intervals reduced
and shivers multiplied and seduced
Springs of the Garden
wonderfully moistened
the lusty love scape
powerfully opened
Springs found their route
to surface bottomless float
my garden mellowed
delicious with scents
of New Spring
a forgotten trunk
implanted with seeds!

"For the time already past is sufficient for you to have carried out the desire
of the Gentiles, having pursued a course of sensuality, lusts, drunkenness,
carousing, drinking parties and abominable idolatries." (Peter 4.3)

BRIDE OF WINTER PASSION

She is soft
and sings aloft
her hair is white
her heart is a sight

she never wakes up
shivering with cold
her passions clothe her
with the hottest ride.

she dreams and dreams
her eyes full of love
she coos her wildest woes
with wild nests thirsty of twos

she is barren with all desires buried
her touch is cutting and her hands are frozen
her kiss is knify and her lips are parched
she shall wake up
as Summer melts her with passion.

"Soma gave you to the Gandharva, the Gandharva gave you to Agni, O Agni transfer her now to me along with prosperity and progeny." (Atharva Veda 14.2.4)

PART – VIII

SEX AND SIN

LUXURIA ET CARITAS

"Son of Man, there were two women, daughters of one mother; and they played the harlot in Egypt. In their youth their breasts were pressed and their virgin bosom was handled.

Their names were Oholah the elder and Oholibah her sister. They bore sons and daughters. Samaria is Oholah and Jerusalem is Oholibah. Oholah lusted after her lovers, her neighbors, governors and officials, all of them desirable young men, horsemen riding on horses. She bestowed her harlotries on them, all their idols she defiled herself. She did not forsake her harlotries from the time in Egypt; for in her youth men had lain with her, and they handled her virgin bosom and poured out their lust on her. Therefore, I gave her into the hand of her lovers, into the hand of the Assyrians, after whom she lusted. They uncovered her nakedness; they took her sons and daughters, but they slew her with the sword. Thus she became a byword among women, and they executed judgments on her.

Now her sister Oholibah saw this, yet she was more corrupt in her lust than she, and her harlotries were more than the harlotries of her sister. She lusted after the Assyrians, governors and officials. She increased her harlotries. And she saw men portrayed on the wall, images of the Chaldeans portrayed with vermilion, girded with belts on their loins, with flowing turbans on their heads, all of them looking like officers, like the Babylonians in Chaldea, the land of their birth. When she saw them she lusted after them and sent messengers to them in Chaldea. The Babylonians came to her to the bed of love and defiled her with their harlotry. And when she had been defiled by them, she became disgusted with them. She uncovered her harlotries and uncovered her nakedness. Then I became disgusted with her, as I had become disgusted with her sister. Yet she multiplied her harlotries, remembering the days of her youth, when she played the harlot in the land of Egypt. She lusted after their paramours, whose flesh is like the flesh of donkeys and whose issue is like the issue of horses. (Ezekiel 23.1-21)

SEX AND SIN

If a poet is not romantic
if he has not done that
what you call sin
yet do it daily
for such painters and poets
women must strip

strip and you shall see
what inspiration you beget
to be a poet painter perfect
to be able to visualise
what within veils and veils
of outer clothing lies

how can you compare
a rose with a lotus
how will you ever smell
nature's true fragrance
and enjoy her aromas
unless you have enjoyed
a delicious woman

No, not in lust alone
but love true
followed by lust too

else what kind of a poet
will ever be you
unless you have

your mind juiced
and lovely desires induced

only then can you be
a love poet like me
ask me what sex
and sin is
all of you must
not hypocrites be

Love a woman
and then see
how poetry flows
from you to me

"For this is the will of God, your sanctification: that you should abstain from
sexual immorality; that each of you should know how to possess his own
vessel in sanctification and honor, not in passion of lust, like the Gentiles
who do not know God." **(Thessalonians 4:3-5)**

"O wives of the Prophet! Whoever of you commits an open illegal **sex**ual
intercourse, the torment for her will be doubled, and that is ever easy for
Allah." (سورة الأحزاب, Al-Ahzaab 33.30)

LOVE IN OVAL OFFICE

Monica curves appealing bonnie
vital stat lithe glib gait
World's powerful Prez
Internally itching
Priming defusing psyche
To grab seize clutch
The fleshy cuisine
Propelled by 'Power aphrodisiac'
Above diaphragm line
Below the navel line
Of missy Monica
Epicenter of Paparazzi
Prez's esurient lenses' zoom-ins.
Glossy slippery
Page Three
Burps out slimy cuisine
For voyeurism
crispy piping hottie
Prez zooms out
Dilated pupils itching
Inching for light free entry
For photic lick lap
In nympholepsy
In opalescent Oval Office
Idiot ID dictates Prez
Coarsely have it n ow
And manhandle
Man's handle
With raw brutality
Snooping prying
Like it or not

Programmed sniffer dogs
Drooling to smear
That feminine odor ooh-la-la
Florid Afghan hounds
With libidinal taste buds
For coarse flesh combing
Snaffle harpooning
Fusillade cartilage cartridges
Deep into recess
of Missy's pouchie
of primitive algae
For benign to bloom
Malign to doom
Hey all stand up
Discover therapeutic purging
Of Gynaecomania, Aidomania
Timeless barbarism
Female cannibalism?
Not for our survival
But their survival
For social sanitization
Through cowardly spine
Hillary forgives
Out of strategic necessity
For sure we know it.
Make it not Modus Vivendi.

"And the two persons (man and woman) among you who commit illegal **sex**ual intercourse, hurt them both. And if they repent and do righteous good deeds, leave them alone. Surely, Allah is ever all-forgiving and most merciful." (سورة النساء, An-Nisaa 4.16)

SEXY POET ARTIST

All artists are lovers first
they kiss....
never miss

Pierce
then tear the canvas
gals in tears

he fixes her soul
solely
on silk only

revealing the camouflaged
hole and sole
the whole
where he
loved
it most

then only will others peel
and love of the ardent artist feel
ask the gal of Titanic
how she felt it

once only!
ere the sinking of the ship
became an everlasting memory

so be it...

BEST FRIEND TOOK HIS GF

Why Oldies brood there is no use
to keep clinging to the past
like embracing a lamp post
but to move on the world's moving fast
unlike in times so old
now lust alone is foremost

where is she?
she was to be on a date with me
but my best friend winked at her
and there she spent the night
with him….drinking
and merry-making

I had to wait outside
but she never came
she returned to him...
he had a car
and all the money
I had not a penny

So lust and thrust survive today
no one can do a thing
but twiddle thumbs
and fingers thin...

Times have changed so
kids don't know their biological father
moms remarry, and re-mother

as they are not used to loneliness
step pops sleep with step kids
and impregnate
such sad story
and it happens, imagine

family norm you speak of is buried
it's time you packed up too
and got remarried,
if there be a need

kids can no longer
their parents feed?

"My child, I do not know what your family name is. In my youthful days, when I moved around as a maid servant, then I got you. Hence I do not know your family name. My name is Jabala and your name is Satyakama. You may therefore call yourself Satyakama Jabala." (Chandogya Upanishad 4.4.2)

SEX IS LIFE

world has never called sex as sin
ask them how they came
about unless parents sexed
and how will the population move forward
and replace the dead without sex

those who are unable to marry
or those who cannot afford a woman
as a girl friend
or those who only sex
secretly
may call sex as sin

the worlds is a-changing openly
guys sex with guys to evade
responsibility
gals sex with gals
and you brand them as lesbian
so how does it matter
they don't have to have babies

but then what else is the purpose of life
if men and women don't have sex

it relieves all tensions and avoids prostate cancers
women if they love they must help their masters
sex is the most joyous creation
God had given to all human
you introduced them as Adam and Eve

we all still believe...

Sex is the choicest gift
given by the unknown Creator
to all whom we call human and animal

we all love sex and must do
if we wish happiness too

"Then he washes his hands, fills the water vessel, and sprinkles her thrice
with that water, saying "Get up from here, and find another young woman
with a husband." (Brihad 6.4.19)

SCENT OF A WOMAN

Your poem depicts sex mostly
here you loved mommy
and now nature truly

do read some of me

my body smells
fruitfully

of apples
oranges
and
peaches

rosy cheeks
nectarish juices
as you pluck off
them easily

as you did once
solilolquily
and
you know it

"And those of your women who commit illegal **sex**ual intercourse, take the evidence of four witnesses from amongst you against them; and if they testify, confine those women to houses until death comes to them or Allah ordains for them some other way." (سورة النساء, An-Nisaa 4.15)

OO MA DOGGIE

And I love dogs
more than human
they tell me they love me so much
and
then my dog gets his ball
he tells me
down the stairs shall we

then when he wants cool water
he takes me to bathroom door
and hits me politely with his nose

after a cool drink
if he is again thirsty
wants cold water from fridge

pulls me and stops at the fridge door
Dumb man
Don't you know...

More about a dog later
who saved my life, thirteen years ago
when the vet told me, in two hours he dies
Who I asked?
my dog or you
my dog survived
I lived
Vet smiled

HOMO ERECTUS

Homing in instincts
Take seed in heart
Hombre on hombre
Before came woman
It was sin of man

How many erections
A peacock shall have
Is written in his eyes
A thousand eyes
On the peacock's tail
Spine up Homo
Erectus
All along your spine
Seed shooters
Erect stand
Love's hour
Is well at hand

Hen shall give way
Cock will have his say
Cockiness deliver
Love's hour is near

"Verily, you practise your **lust**s on men instead of women. Nay, but you are a people transgressing beyond bounds by committing great sins." (سورة الأعراف, Al-A'raaf 7.81)

"Do you practise your **lust**s on men instead of women? Nay, but you are a people who behave senselessly." (سورة النمل, An-Naml 27.55)

MAN BUTTERFLY

A Mushroom
has no room
for thoughts

it has got
only moments to sort
not hours for thought
just split second to rot

in the ageless life
when eternity speaks of strife
butterfly spends but a day
mushroom some watery way

some men are mushrooms
they have messages groomed
but live in hived rooms
in silence they come
and unwreathed they go

some like butterfly
flash across many hearts
with colours vibrant and spots
one flew into my garden
smelling of blossoms of Spring
and fluttered into my passions
caressing here, caressing there
the poets said....beware.

I AM PREGNANT

Love was born in my heart
when I stepped out of bounds
it was raining passionately
My wet heart palpitated;
crazy thoughts pumped my senses

small grass it was
I did not sense at first
by the time the scent
it multiplied and haunted mine
the haunted hunt
and my silent hut
I placed my heart
inside the silent hut
and stopped to talk
talking within
all emotions
wiped with one sweep
of hands
the lips betrayed
the looks beguiled
yet, silently I strolled
I AM PREGNANT
my baby I dreamt.......

"Now the wife whom he desires with the thought "May she conceive", after inserting his member in her and joining mouth to mouth, he should inhale and exhale, repeating the following mantra "With power, with semen, I deposit the semen from you." Thus she verily becomes pregnant." (Brihadaranyak Upanishad 6.4.11)

RAPE OF MY VIRGIN SONG

she was innocent
smiling coyly
talking sweet
hugging softly
winking happily
and tasting lovely
they raped the poem girl
they took away her frock
and untied her petticoats
and tore apart her panties
and forced her to lie
upon a thorny bed
and mantled upon her bleeding core
and made her weep and sob with grief
the new genre of poets
they in the name of poetry
rape her and loot her beauties
and stuff with vulgar weeds
my dear poet virgin
adulterated in the hearts of men
who call their creations poetry.

MAN AND WOMAN

Man - born to create
the first bell
the first act
the first choice
male seeded to seed
it's God will, it succeeds

Woman – the fertile land
with rich alluvial plains
rivulets gurgling
peaks busting
sprouting globe
suckling probes
the answer to his question
quotation to his function
the egging nuisance
the eagling nuance
a tempting lure,
an itching deceit
nature's illusion
natural illustration
she is, he is
she was, he was
in her body she held him
in her spell she halved him

He rapes to Victory
she escapes to adultery
He seeks to place
she is already misplaced.

PRETTY GIRLS POETRY

Smiling girls

I will get back to you
as I have seen
Chandigarh too

on the lake go far and wide
there you will find
what alone one can safely find
at Bombay's Nari-man Point====))))>>- - -

gals give in... ((^))
then they can't cry
they have to smile :))
and now
you also know why

lipsticks perfumes
and wine is fine

I have been around the world
in the West they do not hide
and they continue to enjoy
many a ride

in the East they only smile
as it's all that is left for them
as guys fling and take away
the diamond ring...((^))

what else can gals do
but smile :))
and tell the whole
wide world will you

as you also smiled
at least once maybe
lovely virgin poetry
and pretty girls I can see

many a gals do
and did smile
along with thee
so do not worry
don't smile for me

"Marriage is to be held in honor among all, and the marriage bed is to be undefiled; for fornicators and adulterers God will judge." **(Hebrews 13:4)**

GUYS AND GALS

gals have one brain
and a heart
and
they use both together

guys have two heads
and deceitful heart
they don't use all together
but mostly use
their lower

I thought all gals by now knew
having experienced the net
volatile as it may be
they often have seen guys
scream
for love only
then having poured all
they scram

that's why
I always tell gals
play safe
use condoms

but none listens
till becomes full their tummy
whose is it he asks?
she can't say yours
and he knows

so play safe
from this love game

as your maternity
is a mere fact only
paternity is hearsay
if I may say
listen or not
'tis your will
God IF ANY

"Can a man take fire in his bosom And his clothes not be burned? Or can a man walk on hot coals And his feet not be scorched?" (Proverbs 6.27-28)

"He was not happy. He desired a mate. He made himself as big as a man and woman embracing each other. And then he parted his body into two. From that emerged husband and wife. This body is one-half of oneself, like one of the two halves of a split pea. This space is filled by wife. He was united with her. From that man was born." (Brihad 1.4.3)

IF LOVE NOT GIVEN

Why fire of tune
Ignite in my soul
Why lulu love
Deluge you in my soul?
Why glittery starry garland
Decor you on my neck?
Why touch-travel
O'er my soul
Like rill breeze?
Why vermillion red
Nascent Sun God
Gander at me from east?
Why sway me
By bedecking smile
Like refulgent sky?
Why touch me
Like blooming buds
Smiling at me?
How I'll embosom
Encrypt bind moor
Your vast euphony
Riches rapture rhapsodic
In my wee bosom
If love not given?
Your entire floral love décor
How I'll keep wreath
If love not
Given in my soul?
Why keep me
Pale placid turbid
Instead florid limpid

If love not
Given in my soul
In towering
Pellucid teemingness?

If love not given…

Shall I commit sin?

"If she do not give in, let him, as he likes, bribe her (with presents). And if she then do not give in, let him, as he likes, beat her with a stick or with his hand, and overcome her, saying: "With manly strength and glory I take away thy glory,"—and thus she becomes unglorious." (Brihadaranyak Upanishad 6.4.7)

"It is what comes from inside that defiles you. For from within, out of a person's heart, come evil thoughts, sexual immorality, theft, murder, adultery, greed, wickedness, deceit, lustful desires, envy, slander, pride, and foolishness. All these vile things come from within; they are what defile you."' **(Mark 7:20-23)**

PART – IX

THE KISS OF LIFE

FROM LIP TO LAPS
LAP TO LIPS

HOUSE OF MY BELOVED

Whatever you give, you receive in thousand folds. If you give with a pure heart and a pure mind with pure intentions, when you are sharing your love, your whole being will be flooded with that Love.

Now I know, when I met you, that there is this god whom I had prayed all these days. See, with meeting you the whole thing is over. Now living is the plum of cake. You are asking will I eat the cake or not. See, if I eat it will be finished. So I will only lick and keep on licking so that the cake is okay. I can have the cake and lick the cake.

I want to go to my Beloved's house and die there itself, never to come back again. But when you go to the moon, you will realise that moon is like earth only.....

Love is not mine, neither yours, you cannot possess it, nor can you dispossess it. Every pure mind is permeable to love that flows through it. Like water that runs across when there are no dams, like rivers that flow through forests and wilds, love just flows through hearts when there is no barrier.

RECIPE OF MY FIRST KISS

'Why you',
Dame says,
'Fear hiss
In first kiss? '

~ DAME RECIPING ~

[1] Recipe of
Lip-Lock liquor
Brewing in
5 square centimeter
Lip arena beauty emitter.

[2] Adding: ~
Pentabyte of evocation,
Giga calorie of
Ebullient emotion,
Zillion luxe of imagination.
.

[3] Hues of lips'
Are crisscrossing
Tongues' balleting
Mouth fresheners'
Fragrance swapping
Saliva immixing
[Of 10 ml LOL!].

~ A FEW MINUTES AFTER ~

Propinquity... Proximity...Closing
Nearing n' togethering

Passionate conjoining
Heart beats merging
Pooch-ing n' Pooch-ing
Lips splicing, Quivering, fluttering.
.

Hiked adrenaline
Feelings steeping
Deepening n' diving
Smothering enlivening
Euphoriant levitating.

Voluptuous liquid firing
Every cells dancing
Flutter n' quivering
Tipsiness joyous greening
Infatuation drinking
Unioned lapping
Solace gulping.

~ FINALLY ~

Dame says,
Hey Beau
First kiss
Why you
Fear hiss?
No: Its flowery bliss.

Happened like must
Juxtaposition of
Four lips in trust.

KISS AND CARESS ME

In the most innocent forms I crave for you
In my evening I like to take walk with you
till dusk blesses you and me
with its mild tranquil red rays

Then shall we hold our hands and walk
along this shore smiling to each other
and know that we are in intimate love.

I like to turn to you and look into your eyes.
Kiss me on my forehead and caress my hair
Touch my eyelids and tell me that I am pretty
Such simple things of love I crave for now

Won't you come to me to say goodnight
with the gleaming light in your eyes.
Then I know that you really love me
and not there simply for my body.

I want to fall asleep in your arms.
These are painful nights for me
since I know I will not live for long.
Cancer eats my cells up with ferocity.

When you take me in my arms
I see your eyes get filled
and you tell me without words
that you love and still adore me.

What more does a woman need?
What more does a woman need

KISS WITH CLOSED EYES

most men and women
kiss with eyes closed

they imagine or recall
the last kiss which exposed

a bundle of joy
as lips did explode

all kiss with closed eyes
I suppose
all gals and guys

even same sex do kiss
like you and I

normal ones do kiss
like only this miss....

so kiss on regardless will you
with closed eyes surely will do

"Her strength is his desire, his pleasure. Her passion and fortitude make her excellent in his eyes." (Proverbs 31,10, 29)

COME KISS ME

When a young gal begins to flower
hour by hour
for kisses
lips are open like this
a lovely open to devour

Come enjoy my kisses
I gave when much younger
Kiss me darling
enjoy my kisses
Of kisses I'm hungry fan
Why, Why, O Why
Kisses like yours

When No is in your pocket
try and convert it to a yes
ask a gal for a kiss
she will say no
ask again
she will smile

next time just smile
she will offer her lips
just try
kiss me darling
Kiss me doll
Kiss me doll
say all we

Kiss me darling
kiss me like this

okay just say yes
kiss me like this

Kiss me darling
What's a kiss?
just exchange of bacteria
yours will kill mine
and when lovers kiss
'tis fine

but stolen kisses
last beyond a lifetime

enjoy my kisses
mine alone
one more time
ok say all guys
my alone one more time

Hopefully
we all shall kiss
and die
in the eyes of those
in lust only who fly

Kiss me I'm a hungry fan
anyone for a kiss
say yes
for a kiss
I am feeling jealous man
anyone can kiss me
man or woman...
Of kisses I'm a hungry fan

why do those
whom I love
kisses don't fly towards me
they give it to others
just to tease me

Why, Why, O Why
this is all about a kiss hey guys
this is all about a kiss hey gals

Why, Why, O Why

why
take it for granted
it's just a kiss
a mirage of moms own
a mirage of moms
very own

Love kisses like yours
kisses like yours hi
thanks
Kisses like yours
best kisseseurs
sexy best kisseseurs

kisses like yours
with such a desire
within any gal
you will ignite a fire

like dynamite

but take care
kisses and mostly
Frenchies
tell the liquids are now flowing
everywhere
in more secret zones
none else can know

except the two
who do

Ooooo Kissssss

Kiss is the key to the lock
all human beings finally seek
then kisses fade away
as the locks

just later open up to
by the passers ways
you have so experienced too
kisses are initially
to lovers woo

ere they finally do
what kisses are expected to

"Together we participate in the act of procreation, may you conceive, may
a child be born without deficiency, with all its limbs, not blind, not lame, not
afflicted by demons." (Rg Veda 10.184.1-3)

KISS ME NOW

When you blunder
The world does thunder
When you light a flickering candle
lightening precedes it
and as you open your lips
clouds burst and it rains
drips your tight dress and unveils
what is hidden tightly within

So, kiss me I PRAY
else ask your God
to take my life away

Now of what use on this earth
is my stay
let me silently pass away
or come
and kiss me now
just now today
right away

"Also forbidden are women already married, except those whom your right hands possess. All others are lawful, provided you seek them in **marriage** with Mahr from your property, desiring chastity, not committing illegal sexual intercourse. If after a Mahr is prescribed, you agree mutually, there is no sin on you. Surely, Allah is Ever All-Knowing, All-Wise." (سورة النساء, An-Nisaa 4.24)

HALF KISSED LIPS

Words
half kissed
send out no sounds

lips half missed
dont make
a kissing round

life half lived
does not
complete the sense

anything
half seen
is ill read

But, your heart
though unseen
is both half loved
and fully devoured.

"When a man kisses the upper lip of a woman, while she in return kisses
her lower lip, it is called 'kiss of the upper lip." (Kama Sutra)

BETWEEN CURVES OF A KISS

I found a kiss
implanted upon a miss
i thought it very lovely
for the lips tuned very lively
they licked into
and sticked into
stemmed into
and stormed into
all I could see
was an arch
just a tight parch
with closed looks
and open eyes
none they bothered
nobody they suffered
they were bending
as if they were a single feeling
a curving together
and a cuddling together
the maiden blushed
and the man unblushed
he was passionate
and she all compassionate
she was a delight in arrest
and he with a demand to unrest
undersaid it will be
they spent more than two
hours of time in this wooed
my heart was beating
to watch the figures mouthing
was there nectar in the sacks

of lips burning crimson red
they suckled and sucked
till the world was within hooked
then slowly the petals gave way
and the public presence had a say
they parted to meet in privacy soon
the kiss of life to be implanted cocooned.

"When at night inside a theatre a man comes up to a woman and kisses a finger of her hand if she is standing, or a toe of her foot if she is sitting, or while shampooing her loer's body a woman places her faces in his thigh so as to inflame his passion, and kisses his thigh or toe, it is called a 'demonstrative kiss'. (Kama Sutra)

I WILL KISS THEM BLIND

I want to kiss
a million Orphans
kiss and lick the tears
the blood clot in their hearts
to sponge the bruises
in their thoughts
to tell them
that the rich
are nothing to pitch
that begging
is only a part time thing
that when the muscles
of their softest arms
hardens then the golden harvest
their motherland could harness
i want to kiss the blinds
and remove the blinds
that cling to their minds
and tell them sight
is not external
but deep within the Creator
has dug the magic power for light
and colours and life miracles
to wake up them
from their buried remorses
I want to kiss them
to bloom a thousand roses.

"When a girl touched her lover's lips with her tongue, having shut her own eyes, places her hands on those of her lover, it is called a 'touching kiss'. (Kama Sutra)

SOUL KISS AND FLAMING IRON

A black piece of iron
becomes bright
to become a piece of fire

Behold it
the penetrating fire
shines through iron
that it gives light

Iron does not cease
to be iron
and source of the fire
also retains
its own identity

Fire does not take
the iron into it
but it penetrates
and shines through the iron

It is iron as it was before
so also is the source of fire

And such is the relation
of our soul with God
God penetrates through soul
and dwells in the soul
but soul retains its identity

Soul may not comprehend God
but God comprehends the soul

God does not alter it
from being a soul
but only gives it
its divine source
and glory of the Majesty.

"When a man kisses the reflection of the woman he loves in a mirror, on water or on a polished wall, it is called a 'kiss showing the intention." (Kama Sutra)

"Whosoever intends to perform Hajj should not have **sex**ual relations nor dispute unjustly during the Hajj. For whatever good you do, Allah knows it. Take a provision with you for the journey, but the best provision is righteousness. So fear Me, O men of understanding!" (سورة البقرة, Al-Baqara 2.197)

HONEY KISS

Honey Kiss

Very nice honey and kiss
we all love it
naturally we have to pay
for the honey
the bee's doing labour and dies early
we live longer thereafter...
even the Queen bee '
dies four years thereafter

Only honey labour
bees
have shorter lives
of four months
do you know it?

Humans have a long way to go
and
find how a small honey bee
converts pollen to honey
for you and me

Sweet is honey
like a lovely kiss
we all get from a beautiful miss
but of course for free

You do it daily
you and we all know it...
so for a jar pay,

just for the swift sweetest kiss
Off Honey, you darling miss
Ain't it

Love you do again and again
Kiss, kiss and kiss
till blushes your naughtiest miss...

"When a lover coming home late at night kisses his beloved, who is asleep
on her bed, in order to show her his desire, it is called 'a kiss that awakens'.
On such occasions the woman should pretend to a asleep on her lover's
arrival, so that she may know his intention and obtain respcet from him."
(Kama Sutra)

BIO PSYCHIC KISS

Bio Psychic Kiss
Croons for catharsis.
Mull muse mitosis
Kibosh mute meiosis.
Niminy-piminy noesis
In oomphy orgy osmosis.
Syncretistic synthesis
Open splashy sluice
Bask blottoed bliss.
En fête relish éclat
Zippy zesty zygosis.
Join with Gen Next
In smooch symbiosis

Of Bio-Psychic Kiss!

"When one of the lovers takes both the kips of the other between his or her own, it is called 'a clasping kiss'. A woman will receive such a kiss only from a man who has no moustache. During such kiss if one of the lovers touches the teeth, tongue or palate of the other with tongue, then it is called 'war of the tongues'. (Kama Sutra)

"Blessed are those who guard their modesty, chastity and private parts, from illegal **sex**ual acts." (سورة المؤمنون, Al-Muminoon 23.5)

KISS ON NAKED SNOW

That kisses in the naked snow
will kill many
hope you know
mostly men vie
and
gals sigh
who will kiss this way and why

I shall place my self on the altar of love,
if someone can come and kiss me
the way you two do above.

I love kisses what can I now do
I am sans breath and love too
as my kisses are now like probing poison
a misadventure
now no one kisses me here or there
but I love all those who still kiss
the way we did dear miss...

I can feel your kiss
as my spine shivers
I quiver
Alas at some point of age
we have to deliver
the realities of love
that life does deliver...
kissers we were

KISS ME TONIGHT

Hold me tonight
Ooooo hold me tight
my love as I hold you tonight
for many a night
as tight
so that you may never forget
how I did hold you ever yet

but hold me tonight
as in broad day light
you kissed me on my lips slight
hold me tight
and
let the kiss be a delight
of this night
one we must never forget
ever right

as a kiss of love
hold on to my lips
coming out from sweet nectar
hold me tonight
as you have held me
never
but not as tight as ever.

Just keep holding me tight
My love just for tonight....

PART – X

TEMPLE OF LOVE

PROMISES OF ETERNITY

WRATH OF GOD

For even though they knew God, they did not honour Him as God or give thanks, but they became futile in their speculations, and their foolish heart was darkened.

Professing to be wise, they became fools, and exchanged the glory of the incorruptible God for an image in the form of corruptible man and of birds and four-footed animals and crawling creatures.

Therefore God gave them over in the lusts of their hearts to impurity, so that their bodies would be dishonored among them.

For they exchanged the truth of God for a lie, and worshiped and served the creature rather than the Creator, who is blessed forever. Amen.

For this reason God gave them over to degrading passions; for their women exchanged the natural function for that which is unnatural, and in the same way also the men abandoned the natural function of the woman and burned in their desire toward one another, men with men committing indecent acts and receiving in their own persons the due penalty of their error. (Romans 1.21-27)

BIRDS OF PASSION

It is a green mirror
rippled by every splash
every bird of passion
leaves lovely curls in the ocean
birds of love mates
in the cool branches aside
dip dip dip there goes the heron
happily drenched it soaks its wings
like a fully open fan feasting my sight
the pond is full of mysteries
the more you look at it, the deeper it touches the soul
and the soul is the deepest portion of heart
where nothing but purity and innocence sleeps
There is a magic lantern deep within the pond
it is illuminant from dawn to dusk resplendent
its cooling and beautiful to sight
Magic birds twitter along its side.

"He created you from a single person Adam, and then created from him Eve, so that he might enjoy the pleasure of living with her. When he had **sex**ual relation with her, she became pregnant and she carried it about lightly. But when it became heavy, they both invoked Allah, saying : "If You give us a noble child, we shall be grateful." (سورة الأعراف, Al-A'raaf 7.189)

PASSION OF CHRIST

Painted faces
lovely smiles
sweet kisses
scented napkins
shameless affairs
senseless passions
full moon nights
lusted after
all ends
she has landed

the Cuckoo no more Coos
the melody heart wringing
it has fully stopped. Full stop.
suddenly silence empowered
fullness flows
moon is full or new
now who cares
she has swam across the sky
like a miraculous will
she swept across window sill
the string of films
that whipped up the sleeping harmones
gone all titillating temptations statued
paralysed are all jazz effects
stoned are all starry emulsions
since she has sat upon the green olive tree
Now Cuckoo shall no more Coo
the snapping pain that killed the melting heart
it shall no more be heard
his life mate has honoured

the unkept nuptial bed
now no poetic addresses
no formal ridiculous sufferings
for good the bell has chimed
gates of heavens open wide
Christ is calling pair after pair
O children enter my heavens
darlings come hand in hand
paradise is a dream all divine.

"Now those who belong to Christ Jesus have crucified the flesh with its
passions and desires." (Galatians 5.24)

HONEY BEE IN HORNET'S NEST

Lit from within
the heart glows;
deep red delight
pinked by golden light.
The hands of babies
all soft and fragile
tender beguiles
the energy beneath

touched by the slender fingers
a million heads popped eager
the halo of love
smiled far behind.

Zoomed to visibility
every minute hair stars
bloomed to beauty
A new flower-a rarity.

Passerby peep not inside
two bees are sucking honey
they may sting you thorny
stir up not a hornet's nest
let the lovers bed honey chest.

"The characteristics of manhood consist of roughness and impetuosity, while weakness, tenderness, sensibility and an inclination to turn away from unpleasant things are the distinguishing marks of womanhood. In the excitement of passion sometimes contrary results appear, but these do not last long." (Kama Sutra)

BRIDE IN LOVERS' POND

Green mirrors they are
cool and fresh and pure
azure sky peeps into them
arrowing storks dip into;

Ripples are their expressions
modestly they wriggle within
when breeze touches their virgin lips
shivers run down their circling tips.

Ponds are a beauty, rare beauty
the tiny fishes schooling round
king fishers meditating around
the nostalgia they swell abound.

Clad by fauna of greenery
pebbled deep with velvetty moss beds
ponds speak out legends of love
modest witnesses of moon lit passions.

They storm lusts and lightning urges
they echo the world of birds in love
secretly lap the beauties of nature
treasure sweet rains from every monsoon

Ponds are brides of many lovers
skies and clouds and birds and breeze
all tempt her girlish chuckles

Through the binocular green looks
she says stories

of birds mated, egging, breeding, cooing
the world of love that swarms around
the cool cool pond love whispering fond
deeply lost and drowned in its well
are wandering hearts full of wet memories.

"If a man's wife has a lover and the husband hates him, let him place fire
by an unbaked jar, spread a layer of arrows in inverse order, anoint these
three arrow-heads with butter in inverse order, and sacrifice, saying: "Thou
hast sacrificed in my fire, I take away thy up and down breathing."

"Thou hast sacrificed in my fire, I take away thy sons and cattle."

"Thou hast sacrificed in my fire, I take away thy hope and expectation, I
here."

He whom a Brahmana who knows this curses, departs from this world
without strength and without good works. Therefore let no one wish even
for sport with the wife of a Srotriya who knows this, for he who knows this,
is a dangerous enemy." (Brihadaranyak Upanishad 6.4.12)

HEART BEATS OF LOVE

Let not anyone hurt your heart
let it beat as fast
as when someone
plants a kiss
or
you are running a marathon
let it be that fast

keep no fast
hearts which love
only beat till they last

let it be fast
your lovers will come equally that fast
and
the breeze will never last

as your hearts beat run faster than fast
Let your lovers know
only you will last
ere they are gone past

heart beat I can also hear
thug, thug, thug
is that yours or mine
my poetess dear!

"Blows with the fist should be given on the back of the woman while she is sitting on the lap of the man, and she should give blows in return, making cooing and weeping sounds." (Kama Sutra)

PRAGMATIC LOVE

We must all be pragmatic
youth is like an
apple
enjoy it fully
else
it will sap only

take life as it comes

only be happy
youth is still lovely
at any age

irrespective of physicality

JUST
think you are young still
as I do still...

enjoy every moment of life
every bit
and

do the things you were born to do

sex will make a guy of you too
and save your prostrate
also wifey will be happy

longer lasting marriage
(UNLESS YOU WANT MORE THAN ONE)

no divorces
don't be SAD nor MAD

less medical bills
save your money
avoid here and there
looking around

ILLS

Love still...

Live happily
like me at @73
LOL
any age
I could be....
come and see
okay
just read me

Call from a LOG distance
from poet me

"Then he embraces her, and says: "I am Breath), thou art Speech. Thou
art Speech), I am Breath). I am Sama, thou art Rik. I am the sky, thou art
the earth. Come, let us strive together, that a male child may be begotten."
(Brihadaranyak Upanishad 6.4.20)

"When a woman kisses her lover while he is engaged in business, or
quarelling with her, or looking at something else, so that his mind may be
turned away, it is called a 'kiss that turns away'. (Kama Sutra)

DIGITAL LOVE

Mouse
Mouse
take me
to my Spouse

face I read
from words you feed
emotions I figure
from adjectives of choice

My mail box
Flooded
your messages
invisibly pining

for me to attach
and kiss off replies
heart beats
as dawn breaks

unseens,
unknowns,
reading hearts
and readymade thoughts

A beautiful world
webbing us into
falling prey
Love Spidered...

TELEPATHIC LOVE

Said You
what I thought
replied
I from your heart

touch me
untouched
softly you looked
and pressed me with eyes.

looking into
I can feel
you are watching
my secret passions

stunning me
you turned aside
and made my emotions
topsy-turvy.

some can telepathise
their feelings into you
and creep inside
your innermost
relaxing as a King.

The woman whom he desires with the thought : "May she not conceive"- after inserting the member in her and joining mouth to mouth, he should inhale and exhale, repeating the mantra: "with power, with semen, I reclaim the semen from you." (Brihad 6.4.10)

DOVE'S LOVE

is dove
the symbol of love
nesting for a single mate
resting with singled taste

in the past when they loved
they had faith in their hearts
chaste were the women
who had no counterparts;
and men counted more
the maid within
jewelling the maid without,

now they say
love is bedding
no beads please
only seeds with ease
mothers are no more
angels from heavens
any man can litter
fathers father their fatherless grandsons
mothers wife their wifeless young sons
they say they too love
those who buy the same packs
to bed a wife, a daughter
and a wayside junk

"Who is giving what and to whom? Love is the Giver and Love the
Receiver. Love has entered into Ocean of Being. Through Love I receive
you. O Love all this is for you." (Taittiriya 3.10.1.4) (Atharva 3.29.7)

MY ROOM IN GROOM'S HEART

I have a room
in your heart
I swept it with a groom
made of sentiments intact

I have a chair in your care
I sit upon it and watch with queer
the world you walk across
I too skate down your emotional straws

I have a mirror in your care
which reflects the beauty found everywhere
green and blue, birds and trees
fragrant seasons and fashioned weathers

I have a way in your heart
that I cross every moment of bark
when I beat retreat from the world around
I take refuge on the way of larks

I have a smile inside your looks
a smile that instantly changes its hooks
and meets me in comforting tongues
to cheer me up when I sink into the glooms

I have a hand extending from you
when I drown to catch that fast
to touch it to forget the numb feelings past
to rub it to warm up my freezing body parts....

MY SECRET ROOM IN YOU

My Secret Room
is ever within you
where I share my feelings
emotions soft and strong
deep within the unseen cavities
in caskets of golden colours
I store my passions and longings
and my love's fervour
within your body I seek my desire
within your heart my reflections dear...

"The husband receives his wife from the gods, he does not wed her according to his own will; in order to please the gods he must always support her as long as she is faithful to him. (Manu Smriti 9.95)

THE WOMAN OCEAN

Fascinated,
into forbidden cities
he advented
lured by the scent
of something new
that chilled his spine
and charmed his sinews

a lovely vision
a sight of matchless perfection
the whole world curved
and Oceans exploded
the form that he explored
lent him speechless
and he adored

the way she walked
the way she talked
the looks, the hips, the legs,
the tresses of black in bold
the timeless beauty
that fountained
from that form of time

A splash of lightning
it struck him with the apple
through his nameless muscles supple

he underwent a transformation
and earth got a formation

a pearling love
pristine and doved
textured and domed
moist and succulent
with myriad warm rays
of heavenly soft scents

from the seeded fruits of passion
floating the man into a new Ocean....

of woman love

"She dresses herself with strength, and makes her arms strong." (Proverbs
31.17)

"He addresses the mother of the baby : "Thou art Ila Maitravaruni. Thou
art a strong woman. Be thou blessed with strong children thou who hast
blessed me with a strong child." (Brihad 6.4.28)

AFTER AGES I MET A MAN

When I woke up
my heart sighed
yet another dawn
some vessels to wash
clothes to Iron
food to cook
and floors to sweep
everyday when I get up
same thoughts loot the dawn
I wake up wondering
if I could sleep a little more
and why the world of sleeps was secure more......

Today,
as I ended up the night
with the alarm of my cell
I sprang up
like a rubber ball
though my aches
snowballed halting me fast
ache or no ache
I danced to Kitchen
ideas of breakfast
bulbed in many colours
I was singing into washing vessels
I was humming when I Ironed the clothes
there was some secret
somebody said some magic words
as if they have changed my world

Yes, yesterday I met a man
after ages I met him again
he was there when I was a girl
now, ages since I met him again
he just smiled at me
and shaked my heart
just shaked my heart
and tumbled down the cascades of thoughts
of love and emotions of the past
oh sweetly did I came to life
suddenly I started feeling I am living
in my Zeroed life
somebody sprouted A Meaning
and I wanted to shout aloud
to the bloody empty heads around
that I have somebody now
to love, to cherish and to share
my feelings about life and living beings....

"There is no one greater in this house than I, and he has withheld nothing from me except you, because you are his wife. How then could I do this great evil and sin against God?" As she spoke to Joseph day after day, he did not listen to her to lie beside her or be with her. Now it happened one day that he went into the house to do his work, and none of the men of the household was there inside. She caught him by his garment, saying, "Lie with me!" And he left his garment in her hand and fled, and went outside." (Genesis 39.10-12)

HIS HEART IS GOLD

Who says of him
Hi, I can't see him
know not his name
nor the colour of his frame
from east or west
blessed or best
is he a form
of manly storm
or is he a meek
passerby to seek
somebody calls out
I Love You...

I can feel the tender in those words
he sends the message
to ease my pain
and softens the strokes
by adding more refines
his hands are a beauty
every stroke is lofty
the slants are positive
and seldom stops sensitive
yet, I have not seen
this young man of dreams
young or old his heart is of gold
he sings into my lungs
and ekes out a song
from my voice out of my lips
I am being singed
I hope I could be winged

the breeze brings the charm
kissing the blade of dawn
with the moist love of beds
of grass and smelling buds.

Who says of him
I cannot see him
His heart is of gold
He is my man of old.

"So he left everything he owned in Joseph's charge; and with him there he did not concern himself with anything except the food which he ate. Now Joseph was handsome in form and appearance. It came about after these events that his master's wife looked with desire at Joseph, and she said, "Lie with me." But he refused and said to his master's wife, "Behold, with me here, my master does not concern himself with anything in the house, and he has put all that he owns in my charge." (Genesis 39.6-9)

LONGINGS

One fine morn I met a friend.
She was an Angel
With fluttering wings.
I loved her wings
Her face, her lips
Her eyes, her smile,
Her looks of Innocence.

I can swear
I loved her
more than the Pelican
loved its little ones.

One fine night
She stepped into my bed
Without the wings
Without a cloth.

I wept and wept
She knew not
I longed for
A love beyond the body

"And because of their Jewish disbelief and uttering against Maryam a grave false charge was made that she had committed illegal **sex**ual intercourse." (سورة النساء, An-Nisaa 4.156)

DREAMS ON MY EARTH BED

My bed is on the earth
made of mud with dirt
i wish to sleep along banks
where cooler breeze strokes
and cleaner air streams
my earth is full of scents
of newly blossomed blooms
they open at the nights
with secret chambers in them airtight
nectar in them swells
fills my nostril drums
swimming dreams caress me
with silent touches of soil
and when at midnights
rains slowly stain my eyelashes
with drops of little wetness
they ease me with lovely traces
of smelling earth's Dress.

"But I say, walk by the Spirit, and you will not carry out the desire of the flesh. For the flesh sets its desire against Spirit, and Spirit against the flesh; for these are in opposition to one another, so that you may not do the things that you please. But if you are led by the Spirit, you are not under the Law. (Galatians 5.16-18)

LOVE CEMENTED FORESTS

Forests of cement
if there is any beauty
between
Cement and forest
and
any love between
man and woman
'tis here

let all the waters
not wash it away
Love is very dear
Costly here
part of mother
Earth

"Those who take an oath not to have **sex**ual relation with their wives must wait for four months, and then if they return, verily, Allah is Oft-Forgiving, Most Merciful." (سورة البقرة, Al-Baqara 2.226)

STILL I LOVE YOU
(You said it 10 TIMES)

it seems she needs
to be assured
by love alone
no less any more
in the act lies the cure
than just saying
only ashore

swim with her in the nude
and see she will know everything
between the forests trees
thick or thin
where both of you
would've been
and so much more seen

modify your stance
and I do you assure
more love you will get from her
and much, hopefully much more

all others on the beach
will also you adore
though I hope
she loves you
till yore

LOVE AT THE END OF TUNNEL

It is chilling outside here
glow worms are my only hopes
little do I know
that glow worms are not hot.
rains have wet earth beyond its hold
now, air is cool and heavy with moist bold.
Frogs love the fridges of green
they croak and love-till snake's dream.

I am freezing
my limbs are paining
bones are needling, brains numbing.
no blankets shroud, nor blinking lights appear
I am in a forest full of empty cheers
tears and fears all ice now
I sit and try to doze my nights.

The spears of enemies swirl around
like the giggling baby under elephant's feet
I clap my hands to catch them to ground
I am jittering, my teeth feverish chatting
slowly I slip into icy coma
death penetrates, infiltrating sleep comes
Every bee and butterfly crowd my heap
Poor things I starved their seats.

When love is Spring
Hate is Monsoon
but rains are nice
but chillness has a price
I am depreciated, my value begins at zero

never did I feel that my currency is Greece
I feel the marathon of sperms beginning
rebirth sounds at the end of the tunnel
the train is empty now
maybe I am the first to funnel.

Editor's Note :- Hemangi Sharma wrote it on July 18, 2015. The words
Spring and Monsoon are code names of people in her personal life, which
she had discussed with me in detail.)

"Having sacrificed, he takes out the remaining rice and eats it, and after
having eaten, he gives it to his wife. Then he washes hands, fills a water-
jar, and sprinkles her thrice with it, saying: "Rise O Visvavasu, seek
another blooming girl with her husband." (Brihad 6.4.19)

YOU ARE MY TEMPLE, LORD

I see in you
somebody I left
behind somewhere
as I walked
along the path
invisibly familiar
are your parts
I know not thy face
nor your name
or your person and mine
how they link in twined
but somehow
something in you
reminds me of ages beyond
that your looks
carry within
a mirror flashing me
and mine stored in thine
that I know you very well
without words
you are mine
that though I speak not
yet I can find it
that your looks are wells
of water imaging dwells
of our pasts
that you were there
with me in touch
that I know you more
than this life could store
that some unseen thread

is tying the knot
from heart to heart
that too familiar are you
to pretend a new
I am yours
a part or thing or thought
or component lot
some blood runs in my vein
same as your timeless brain
Do you read me
I know for sure
I am just in you
yes, you are my home
you are my templing lord.

"Let no one say when he is tempted, "I am being tempted by God"; for God cannot be tempted by evil, and He Himself does not tempt anyone. But each one is tempted when he is carried away and enticed by his own lust. Then when lust has conceived, it gives birth to sin; and when sin is accomplished, it brings forth death." (James 1.13-15)

EPILOGUE

HEMANGI SHARMA

AS SMT LALITHA IYER

I AM NOT FAKE

My dear poet friend
It is not a fake ID
Only my pseudonym
And I am not theoretical poet
I am a class one English poet
Though an unconventional poet
An off the cuff instant poet
Name and fame I do not care
I am already established
In many languages
In many formats

Shakespeare was not in life
A follower like you my dear
He was a poem in flow
You must have your own DNA
To become a poet of substance
I have been to a poetry academy
Where they stripped me nude
And now my poems they salute

HEMANGI SHARMA

AS SMT LALITHA IYER

It was in the year 2007 when for the first time I noticed certain unusual activities while browsing the internet. I saw several social media posts by different persons with different IDs which had the same underlying pattern and digital footprint. When I tried to follow some of those posts, I started receiving similar posts in my own e-mail ID as spam messages. Although I found it quite baffling, I thought it could be just a coincidence.

Then in 2009 a woman started stacking me online and also over phone. I received a series of calls from a woman claiming to be one Swapna from Bangalore. Sometimes this woman told me that she was working as an executive at Google India office, while at other times she said she was working at Facebook. The woman started calling me from different phone numbers, each time giving a different name such as Swapna, Jyoti, Kiran, Savita, Kavita etc. It was quite obvious that it was the same woman, since the voice, accent, style and intonation was the same. It was also obvious that she was stalking me for an ulterior motive, since a Google or Facebook executive would have little to do with someone like me who had hardly any presence on social media.

During the years 2011 and 2012 there was a marked reduction in the stalking activity of this woman. So I had largely forgotten about those spam calls and messages. But then suddenly in September 2013 a woman named Chitrangdha K Ganesh sent me a message on Poemhunter website. The title of her message read "I am bowled over by your poetic skills". It was very perplexing. I

In August 2013 I had exposed certain fraudulent activities in the online Poemhunter Poetry Competition, in which I was a participant. I found that out of the 100 poems reaching the final, 37 appeared to be the works of same person. The poems showed exquisite craftsmanship and were on wide ranging topics. But all these 37 poems had a typical signature style. Many of these poems had been submitted by poets with similar names such as Prem Kumar, Prem Jyot, Prem123 etc. I had lodged a written complaint with Poemhunter.com website regarding such fraud, but received no response.

When I received the mail from Chitrangdha initially I thought as if the sender had some divine connection with me. But immediately I remembered the Poemhunter fraud, and thought this woman could be connected with that episode. Either the woman herself was the fraudster, or maybe some Poemhunter staff investigating the fraud. So I was wary of disclosing any details about me to this woman.

Although initially I avoided the woman, she kept on sending me her e-mail IDs and mobile numbers, requesting me to share my contact details. Although I was wary of the woman, finally curiosity got the better of me. I did some online chatting with the woman on Poemhunter platform. She introduced herself to me as a freelance worker in the field of advertisement and tourism. However after some time she started contradicting her own statements. Sometimes she said she was a researcher, a student, and IT professional or even a journalist. Sometimes she said she was married, and sometimes unmarried. Sometimes she said she was 39 years old, and at other times 33 or 43.

In April-May 2014 "Chitrangdha" obtained from me my mobile number and called me. In her very first call she told me about her life-long desire to study the Rg Veda and Qu'ran. She also told me that one day she would like to come to my house to study the Veda and Qu'ran with me. I found it quite surprising. Because ever since my childhood I had an unusual interest in the scriptures, and I had particular fascination for the rhythmic mantras of Rg Veda and Sama Veda as well as for the melodious Ayats of Quran as rendered by the Muezzins in mosques.

I developed a very intimate online relationship with this Chitrangdha. She was the first person with whom I had any personal chats online. She exchanged hundreds of messages with me via Facebook, WhatsApp, Poemhunter, SMS and other media. Sometimes she would call me up to ten times in a day. Often she told me that it was her life-long desire to come to my house and spend the rest of her life with me. I found t very strange. I suspected of a past life connection with her.

On June 5, 2015 Chitrangdha revealed to me that her actual name was Hemangi Sharma, and that she was a student at National Institute of Rural Development, Hyderabad. She also admitted that she had been trolling me since 2009 under a series of fake IDs. She said she came to know about me from a person named Basant Kumar Rath, a senior police officer posted in Jammu. This Basant Rath was my childhood friend and had studied with me in the same class up to university level. Hemangi Sharma aka Chitrangdha had been born and brought up in Jammu before she moved to Bangalore and Hyderabad for job.

In July 2015 I met Hemangi Sharma at her office in Hyderabad. She had invited me to participate in the annual convocation ceremony of her institute. She had booked a room for me in her office guest house. I spent two days with her. During those two days she shared with me her life story. She also discussed the hidden secrets of various world scriptures including the Bible and the Qu'ran. The religious philosophies that Hemangi Sharma discussed with me are the same that Lalitha Iyer has described in detail in his Christian poems.

When I met Hemangi Sharma in person she did not admit that she was Lalitha Iyer. But she admitted that she had hundreds of fake IDs. She showed me how she had created multiple Ids by using different mobile phones and SIM cards. But when I asked her to open Chitrangdha's e-mail, she said she had forgotten Chitra's password. When I asked her why she had opened so many fake IDs, she said that she had worked as a marketing executive at Google and Facebook, and that sending spam advertisements to unsuspecting customers was part of her lucrative corporate job. She also said that she had got fed up with that kind of artificial and unethical job, and therefore she had quit the job to pursue a career in rural development.

Initially Hemangi Sharma had shared with me those IDs through whch she had been sending spam mails. But after I came back from Hyderabad, Hemangi Sharma gradually revealed to me her other IDs under which she had posted thousands of poems online. But she did majority of her poetry correspondence with me through the ID of Lalitha Iyer.

Ït was chiefly through the intimate discussion with Lalitha Iyer" "that I realised Hemangi Sharma's true stature as a world class poet. Lalitha became my sparring partner in poetry. Sometimes she would compose an instant poem online and challenge me to respond to her with a poem.

It was quite surprising for me that Hemangi had not published even a single poem under her own name. All her poems had been published under hundreds of pseudonyms like Lalitha Iyer and Anthony Theodore. After introducing me to her poetry, Hemangi Sharma deactivated her original e-mail IDs. So I was forced to correspond with her via her fake IDs. She discussed her poetry with me in great detail over thousands of messages exchanged through such fake IDs. And then one fine day she deleted all her messages to me. That left me with no evidence that she had indeed discussed her poetry with me. However I managed to save a few of those messages as proof of her correspondence with me.

Hemangi Sharma has uploaded thousands of her poems in different languages under hundreds of fake IDs. She is a multi-linguist with scholarly understanding of all major world religions. She has original and unique insights into scriptural truths. One fails to understand why a highly educated spiritual person like her would use so many fake IDs, which is a criminal offence. But then strange are the ways of the devotees of God. She told me she had created the fake IDs when she was working as an executive at Google India and Facebook. The fake IDs were used for sending spam marketing advertisements to unsuspecting potential clients. But pretty soon she got fed up with that kind of job, and left the corporate world. However, after she left the marketing world, she continued to use the fake IDs to publish her poems online without revealing her true identity.

Of course, this is Hemangi Sharma's version. I have no means of verifying the truth in her statements.

When Hemangi Sharma first started corresponding with me, I immediately knew that she was the person behind the hundreds of fake IDs under which she had uploaded her poems. However she admitted to it much later, only after I relentlessly pursued her to know the truth. She has the talent and creativity to write spontaneously in thousands of different styles. But there were certain underlying patterns in all her works. The most common element in her writings is her use of small "i" to denote the first person singular. She purportedly did so to underplay the individual ego in the creative process. But there is still no plausible explanation for the use of thousands of fake IDs. She could have adopted a single pseudonym to mask her identity, but she chose to have thousands. I believe that she wrote under fake IDs to completely dissociate her ego from the creative process. I myself had resorted to such a technique during my student days. I found that the poems I had written under pseudonyms were qualitatively much better than those published under my real name.

Another underlying pattern in Hemangi Sharma's writings is her utter disregard for the conventional rules of grammar. Among all her online avatars, I found Dr Antony Theodore as comparatively more conventional in terms of literal style. Lalitha Iyer was more flexible as a poet. But in her personal correspondence with me, Lalitha threw all grammatical rules to the wind. The poetic freedom can be easily seen by discerning readers.

Yet another frequent feature in Hemangi Sharma's writings is the use of abbreviations, colloquial expressions and liberal use of nouns as verbs and adjectives. For instance she would write "RV Lovers" instead of "Are We in Love". You is abbreviated to "u" in most of her writings. Instead of "more childish", she will simply write "childer". For instance, in one of her letters to me, she wrote "love makes heart become childer".

What makes her art so special is that she makes such unusual expressions quite spontaneously. The reader hardly suspects that she is deliberately doing so.

In addition to "Lalitha Iyer", Hemangi Sharma has also adopted other interesting pseudonyms such as Antony Theodore, Dev Anand, Poet Poet, Sun Princess, April Pearl and a host of other IDs. Antony Theodore is perhaps the most famous amongst all her online avatars. But God alone knows how many fake IDs she has created. She herself told me that she had forgotten most of her IDs and passwords. She has used both male and female names, as well as names from different languages. She has used Hindu names, Christian names and Muslim names. Maybe she did so to identify herself with all humanity irrespective of artificial barriers created by gender, race, caste, language and religion.

But still she could have managed to do all this with 30 or 40 IDs. I really don't know what could have been Hemangi Sharma's real intention in adopting hundreds and thousands of fake IDs. Any discerning reader would have noticed the underlying pattern in the poems written under different IDs. But perhaps nobody pointed it out before I did so. I was the only person who lodged a written complaint regarding her fake IDs. Perhaps Hemangi Sharma deliberately did so with the expectation that someday someone would find out her real identity. Perhaps it was God's design that I would become that person. Or maybe it was Hemangi Sharma's own design – who knows?

Hemangi Sharma had been writing under the ID of Lalitha much before she came in personal contact with me. But her early poems reflected more of pain and sadness rather than romantic love. The tone and tenor of her poetry shifted remarkably to erotic romance after she contacted me. I was not aware of her poetry when she first interacted with me. She was using a number of pseudonyms and it was almost impossible for me to discover her works all by myself. She gradually introduced me to her works poem by poem.

It is pertinent to note that Hemangi Sharma has not published even a single poem in her own name. She had sent me a few blank verses through WhatsApp and Facebook messenger, requesting me to convert them to lyrical poems. But I had not responded to her request at that time. Later she told me that she would share with me her poetry only through a fake ID, since she did not wish to be recognised in public. She had suggested that I should also create a fake ID for the purpose. But I had declined to do so. Instead I created a joint ID with her with the profile name Smt Hemangi Tapan Pradhan. She always loved to be addressed as Shrimati Hemangi, hence that name.

Lalitha Iyer's poetic exchanges with me were through this joint ID of Smt Hemangi Tapan Pradhan. Thousands of messages were exchanged – sometimes 30 to 40 per day. Many messages had accompanying pictures also. Hundreds of people on internet had seen all those exchanges and had praised the surpassing beauty of those instant compositions.

Lalitha has deleted almost all the erotic messages she had shared with me. The messages were in dialogue form and covered a diversity of topics including love, marriage, virtue, sin, religion, Christianity. But the most intense and beautiful poems were on love and eroticism. These poems are full of joy and vivacity as compared to her earlier gloomy poetry. When I look back on all those poetic exchanges, I clearly feel that Lalitha had a premonition regarding her meeting me one day in this life.

Although her profile name was Lalitha Iyer, I used to address her lovingly as Lolita. She also loved this appellation, and had sent me a poem based on Nabokov's character by that mischievous name. Details of my relationship with "Lalitha" (Lolita) can be found in my book "I, She and the Sea".

I never expected that one day she would delete all those lovely messages. I treasured all those lovely compositions. I could retrieve many of those messages. But had I known about her plans, I would have definitely taken screenshots of those messages and pictures so that I could have savoured them in my old age. It is now not possible for me to recreate the magic of that kind of intensity in poetry.

As for evidence I have managed to save only some of my intimate correspondence with "Lalitha Iyer". This saved portion is only a small fraction of the voluminous correspondence she had with me consisting of thousands of text messages and impromptu poems. Almost 95% of my poetry exchanges with Hemangi Sharma had taken place with the ID of Lalitha Iyer. I do not know whether all those deleted messages can be recovered now. If not, it would be a huge personal loss for me.

Tapan Kumar Pradhan
25 December 2020

ABBREVIATIONS

Atharva :- Atharva Veda
Brihad :- Brihandaranyaka Upanishad
Chandogya :- Chhandogya Upanishad
Corinth :- Book of Corinthians, Bible
KamaS :- Kama Sutra of Vatsyayana
Padma :- Padma Purana
Rg :- Rig Veda
Sama :- Sama Veda
Taittir :- Taittiriya Upanishad
Yajur :- Yajur Veda

REFERENCES

Ali, A. Y. (2011). *The Holy Quran*. Global Islamic Publications

Desmond, L. (2011). *The Pleasure Is Mine – Changing Subject of Erotic Science*. **Journal of Indian Philosophy**, 39 (1), 41-62

Doniger, W. (2016). *Redeeming Kama Sutra*. Oxford University Press.

Graham, L. (1995). *A Love Map to His Body*. Redbook Publishers.

Ludo, R. (1985). *The Kama sutra – Vatsyayana's Attitude towards Dharma and Dharma Sastra*, J. of American Oriental Society, 105 (3). 521-23

Rajneesh, O. (2018). *Sex to Superconsciousness*. Full Circle Publishing

Sankaracharya (1950). *Brihadaranyaka Upanishad – Commentary by Shankara* {Tr. By Swami Madhavananda]. Advaita Ashrama, Delhi

Sankaracharya (2010). *Chandogya Upanishad – Commentary by Shankara* [Tr. By Swami Swahananda]. Sri Ramakrishna Math, Delhi

Vatsayana (1961). *Kama Sutra of Vatsyayana – Complete Translation from Original Sanskrit* [Tr. By S C Upadhyaya]. DB Taraporewala.

Yogananda, P. (1995). *God Talks With Arjuna – The Bhagavad Gita*. Self Realisation Fellowship.

Yogananda, P. (2004). *The Second Coming of Christ*. Self Realisation Fellowship

Yogananda, P. (1996). *Wine of the Mystic*. Self Realisation Fellowship.